D0205224

LB 2831.58 .T56 1996
Thompson, David P., 1959-
Motivating others

DATE DUE

BRODART, CO. Cat. No. 23-221-003

Motivating Others

Creating the Conditions

David P. Thompson

EYE ON EDUCATION
P.O. BOX 3113
PRINCETON, NJ 08543
(609) 395–0005
(609) 395–1180 fax

Copyright © 1996 Eye On Education, Inc.
All Rights Reserved.

For information about permission to reproduce selections from this book, write:
Eye On Education, Permissions Dept., P.O. Box 3113, Princeton, NJ 08543

Library of Congress Cataloging-in-Publication Data

Thompson, David P., 1959-
Motivating others : creating the conditions / by David P. Thompson.
p. cm.
Includes bibliographical references.
ISBN 1-883001-25-0
1. School personnel management—United States—Psychological aspects. 2. Motivation in education—United States. 3. Teacher -principal relationships—United States. I. Title.
LB2831.58.T56 1996
370.2'01—dc20 96-5825
CIP

10 9 8 7 6 5 4 3 2 1

Editorial and production services provided by Richard H. Adin Freelance Editorial Services, 9 Orchard Drive, Gardiner, NY 12525 (914-883-5884)

LB
2831.58
.T56
1996

Published by Eye On Education:

Block Scheduling: A Catalyst for Change in High Schools
by Robert Lynn Canady and Michael D. Rettig

Teaching in the Block
edited by Robert Lynn Canady and Michael D. Rettig

Educational Technology: Best Practices from America's Schools
by William C. Bozeman and Donna J. Baumbach

The Educator's Brief Guide to Computers in the Schools
by Eugene F. Provenzo, Jr.

Handbook of Educational Terms and Applications
by Arthur K. Ellis and Jeffrey T. Fouts

Research on Educational Innovations
by Arthur K. Ellis and Jeffrey T. Fouts

Research on School Restructuring
by Arthur K. Ellis and Jeffrey T. Fouts

Hands-on Leadership Tools for Principals
by Ray Calabrese, Gary Short, and Sally Zepeda

The Principal's Edge
by Jack McCall

The Administrator's Guide to School-Community Relations
by George E. Pawlas

Leadership: A Relevant and Realistic Role for Principals
by Gary M. Crow, L. Joseph Matthews, and Lloyd E. McCleary

Organizational Oversight:
Planning and Scheduling for Effectiveness
by David A. Erlandson, Peggy L. Stark, and Sharon M. Ward

Motivating Others: Creating the Conditions
by David P. Thompson

Oral and Nonverbal Expression
by Ivan Muse

The School Portfolio:
A Comprehensive Framework for School Improvement
by Victoria L. Bernhardt

School-to-Work
by Arnold H. Packer and Marion W. Pines

Innovations in Parent and Family Involvement
by William Rioux and Nancy Berla

The Performance Assessment Handbook
Volume 1: Portfolios and Socratic Seminars
by Bil Johnson

The Performance Assessment Handbook
Volume 2: Performances and Exhibitions
by Bil Johnson

Bringing the NCTM Standards to Life
by Lisa B. Owen and Charles E. Lamb

Mathematics the Write Way
by Marilyn S. Neil

Transforming Education Through Total Quality Management: A Practitioner's Guide
by Franklin P. Schargel

Quality and Education: Critical Linkages
by Betty L. McCormick

The Educator's Guide to Implementing Outcomes
by William J. Smith

Schools for All Learners: Beyond the Bell Curve
by Renfro C. Manning

FOREWORD

The School Leadership Library was designed to show practicing and aspiring principals what they should know and be able to do to be effective leaders of their schools. The books in this series were written to answer the question, "How can we improve our schools by improving the effectiveness of our principals?"

Success in the principalship, like in other professions, requires mastery of a knowledge and skills base. One of the goals of the National Policy Board for Educational Administration (sponsored by NAESP, NASSP, AASA, ASCD, NCPEA, UCEA, and other professional organizations) was to define and organize that knowledge and skill base. The result of our efforts was the development of a set of 21 "domains," building blocks representing the core understandings and capabilities required of successful principals.

The 21 domains of knowledge and skills are organized under four broad areas: Functional, Programmatic, Interpersonal and Contextual. They are as follows:

FUNCTIONAL DOMAINS
- Leadership
- Information Collection
- Problem Analysis
- Judgment
- Organizational Oversight
- Implementation
- Delegation

PROGRAMMATIC DOMAINS
- Instruction and the Learning Environment
- Curriculum Design
- Student Guidance and Development
- Staff Development
- Measurement and Evaluation
- Resource Allocation

INTERPERSONAL DOMAINS
- Motivating Others
- Interpersonal Sensitivity
- Oral and Nonverbal Expression
- Written Expression

CONTEXTUAL DOMAINS
- Philosophical and Cultural Values
- Legal and Regulatory Applications
- Policy and Political Influences
- Public Relations

These domains are not discrete, separate entities. Rather, they evolved only for the purpose of providing manageable descriptions of essential content and practice so as to better understand the entire complex role of the principalship. Because human behavior comes in "bunches" rather than neat packages, they are also overlapping pieces of a complex puzzle. Consider the domains as converging streams of behavior that spill over one another's banks but that all contribute to the total reservoir of knowledge and skills required of today's principals.

The School Leadership Library was established by General Editors David Erlandson and Al Wilson to provide a broad examination of the content and skills in all of the domains. The authors of each volume in this series offer concrete and realistic illustrations and examples, along with reflective exercises. You will find their work to be of exceptional merit, illustrating with insight the depth and interconnectedness of the domains. This series provides the fullest, most contemporary, and most useful information available for the preparation and professional development of principals.

Scott D. Thomson
Executive Secretary
National Policy Board for
Educational Administration

If you would like information about how to become a member of the **School Leadership Library**, please contact

Eye On Education
PO Box 3113
Princeton, NJ 08543
(609) 395-0005
(609) 395-1180 FAX

ABOUT THE AUTHOR

David P. Thompson is an assistant professor of educational administration at East Texas State University. He received his Ph.D. in educational administration from Texas A&M University in 1993. His professional interests include job satisfaction and motivation, quantitative research methods, the principalship, and school law.

Immediately prior to his appointment at East Texas State University in 1994, Dr. Thompson was an assistant principal at Westfield High School in the Spring (Texas) Independent School District. In addition, he has been a public school mathematics teacher and coach and a graduate research associate with the Texas A&M School/University Research Collaborative.

For his doctoral dissertation titled "Job Satisfaction: A Synthesis of Research in the *Educational Administration Quarterly*," Dr. Thompson received the outstanding dissertation awards in 1994 from both Division A of the American Educational Research Association and the National Council of Professors of Educational Administration.

PREFACE

It hardly bears repeating that the principal's job is as challenging and demanding as it can possibly be. In fact, the principal's job as a leader is really paradoxical. The principal finds him or herself in the middle of nearly every facet of the school district's educational process. The principal answers to the superintendent (and often times the board), to teachers, students, parents, community members, and, at times, even to the media.

At the same time, the principal is the leader of the building, responsible for all aspects of the school's operation. The principal is the person to whom teachers, parents, students, and community members look for leadership, guidance, stability, and answers to typically complex questions.

Still simultaneously, the principal, as leader of the school, is expected to share this leadership with the school staff (particularly teachers) and with the community served by the school. Across the United States are site-based decision-making teams, school governance councils, and similar structures, put in place (either voluntarily or by legal mandate) to ensure that the voices of stakeholders are heard in the schooling process.

The paradox of the principal's job is obvious. While the principal is the leader, he or she is the servant of those whom he or she leads. In no other facet of the principal's work is this more true than in the area of motivating teachers. No longer is the principal able (or advised) to rely solely (or even predominantly) on the power of the position to energize, direct, and sustain teacher behavior. In fact, the principal *cannot motivate teachers*. Motivation is an internal state; for teachers who have needs for personal and professional growth to experience this internal state, certain conditions must be present in their work. These conditions include opportunities for teachers to utilize and augment their complement of skills, to perform significant and "whole" tasks, to work as colleagues in pursuit of a common vision, to assume responsibility for their work performance, to know how they are performing during the course of their work activities, and to be recognized for performing effectively. The principal, then, becomes the servant of teachers by creating these conditions which can result in this internal state of motivation.

Throughout the book, David Thompson develops this notion of "creating the conditions," which is the first element in the National

Policy Board's definition of the domain of Motivating Others. The entire definition reads:

> Creating conditions that enhance the staff's desire and willingness to focus energy on achieving educational excellence; planning and encouraging participation; facilitating teamwork and collegiality; treating staff as professionals; providing intellectual stimulation; supporting innovation; recognizing and rewarding effective performance; providing feedback, coaching and guidance; providing needed resources; serving as a role model.

With this emphasis on "creating the conditions," Thompson brings the reader through the practical strategies required in motivating others, using the elements of the Policy Board's definition as an outline for his work. He demonstrates that the principal's role in motivation is not so much to personally motivate teachers as it is to create these conditions in teachers' work so that teachers with needs for professional and personal growth can, for themselves, experience their own internal motivation. With these conditions in place, teachers' internal motivation is more likely to be sustained over long periods of time and is less likely to be dependent on the actions and works of the principal.

The author takes what is known about creating these conditions for teacher motivation and applies this knowledge to principals' (and prospective principals') work. Heavily interspersed throughout the book are "real-world" applications which will assist principals in creating these conditions. These applications include best practices of effective principals, checklists, questionnaires, models for decision-making and recognizing effective performance, and action plans. This practical, yet scholarly presentation of the principles of motivation promises genuine assistance for the principal or prospective principal who seeks to develop skill in this domain.

David A. Erlandson
Alfred P. Wilson

Acknowledgments

To say that I was surprised when Dave Erlandson asked me to author this volume would be an understatement. To be sure, there are many others more qualified (many of whom are cited in this book) to speak to principals about teacher motivation. Accordingly, I owe Dave Erlandson my heartfelt gratitude for his confidence in choosing me and his nurturing guidance as this volume unfolded.

In addition, five colleagues acted as "practitioner-editors" in order that they might keep my thoughts and ideas grounded in the real world in which principals operate. These professionals are Julie Combs, principal of Woodrow Wilson Elementary School in the Coppell (Texas) Independent School District; Michael Killian, associate superintendent for instruction in the Lewisville (Texas) Independent School District; Joseph Kopec, principal of Austin High School in the Austin (Texas) Independent School District; Greg McIntyre, assistant principal of A&M Consolidated High School in the College Station (Texas) Independent School District; and Karen Raney, principal of Hubbard Middle School in the Tyler (Texas) Independent School District. I thank each of you for your insightful, substantive comments and for your encouragement.

I am deeply indebted to the support I received from my colleagues at East Texas State University, including Anita Pankake, Frank Lutz, Jim Vornberg, Gwen Schroth, Max Jobe, and RuthAnn Stephens. Thanks for the pep talks, Anita.

Thanks as well go to my mentors and colleagues from Texas A&M University, John Hoyle and Jim McNamara. Your ongoing support and encouragement is truly energizing.

For my grounding in the world of practice, I am deeply grateful to my friends and colleagues from Westfield High School and the Spring Independent School District. Thanks to Ken McKinney, Carm Castoria, Jeannie Heiskell, Cindy Leo, Devery Parker, David Harsch, Larry Wallace, Rex Grozier, Carolyn Boyce, Donna Grant, Bobby Morris, Janice Taylor, Rocky Kirk, Jack Moss, Gordon Anderson, and Rob Smith.

Finally, my deepest gratitude goes to my wife D'Anne, and daughter Rachel Hannah, each to whom this book is dedicated.

Dedication

To
D'Anne, whose encouragement and sacrifices
I am only beginning to appreciate,
and
Rachel Hannah, whose intrinsic motivation
is a constant source of inspiration.

TABLE OF CONTENTS

1

SETTING THE STAGE

It is the middle of the night, actually early on a cold, snowy March Wednesday morning. You look at the clock and it reads 2:30 a.m. You turn over in bed for the umpteenth time and command yourself to go to sleep. It's been an hour since you went to bed, trying carefully not to awaken your spouse. The flood of seemingly random thoughts just won't stop. What a day! The school was abuzz about the girls basketball team's regional championship game. One win and the girls would be going to state. Unfortunately, the dream came crashing down with a last-minute basket which beat the team in triple-overtime. Everyone knows that your team should have won handily; the coach has been under fire all season because the team wasn't winning convincingly. A certain group of influential parents has even been stirring up talk about a new coach. Certainly, this game will not help to douse the fire. Anyway, you didn't get home until 1:00 a.m. because the game was played 100 miles down the road and school buses can't travel at more than 50 miles per hour. On Monday, your two year old daughter learned each of her "A-B-C's" in order; unfortunately, due to Monday evening's board meeting and Wednesday night's Site-Based Decision-making committee meeting, you won't get to hear her utter those precious words until Thursday at the earliest. Oh, that's right. Tomorrow. Does it really start at 5 a.m.? Was it really my idea to schedule a classroom observation for first period with the head of the local teacher's union, who is currently embroiled in a messy grievance with the school district? Will the parents who are mumbling about a new basketball coach be waiting in my office when I arrive? Is the discipline hearing for the learning-disabled son of the band booster club president really tomorrow as well? Will it snow eight inches tonight like the weather forecast predicted? What does all of this have to do with me being the instructional leader of this campus?

Even though this scenario is fictitious (somewhat!), it illustrates the situations that school principals face in trying to lead teachers, students, and parents to the goal of educational excellence, operationally defined as student success. Like the principal in this scenario who finally went to sleep at 3:30 a.m., arose at 5:00 a.m., and helped provide the opportunity for children to achieve that day, something inside of you propels you to do the same thing day in and day out. That something inside of each of you is motivation.

Notice that I said "something inside of you." I truly believe—and not just because "the research" tells us so—that we do not initiate and sustain our behaviors as educators because we anticipate receiving some extrinsic reinforcement such as a paycheck or extra time off during a holiday period. Rather, I believe that we do what we do because we are engaged in a "cause greater than one's self"; that is, we believe that we have the opportunity to make a difference in the lives of our students and our fellow educators. As one elementary school teacher so simply, and yet so eloquently, put it:

> . . . I get satisfaction, I get a lot of love from the kids I teach. I really feel that I have the possibility to make a difference in somebody's life, which to me is worth more than the money, I guess. I mean, certainly you're not in it for the money. And you're not in it for the prestige. And you're not in it for the sense of autonomy, because you don't have much autonomy, in terms of what you want to do. But for what you get from the one-on-one with kids, I don't think anyone could replace that feeling for me personally. (Johnson, as quoted in Sergiovanni, 1992, p. 23).

Something motivated the principal in our scenario to get up and take on another challenging day. Yet, we know that principals do not exist in a vacuum. Principals are, if only by the virtue of their positions, the leaders of our schools. In spite of reform efforts such as shared governance, site-based management, and participative decision-making, one thing seems not to have changed: When all is said and done, the "buck still stops" at the principal's door. As such, the principal is not only responsible for self-motivation, but more importantly is held accountable for the motivation of the school staff and even students.

WHY ANOTHER BOOK ON MOTIVATION?

Good question. In a recent *five-minute* examination of several online databases, I discovered the following. The East Texas State University Library Information System listed over 500 book titles on motivation; the ERIC database indexed nearly 24,000 articles and other documents addressing motivation in one form or another between 1966 and 1995. Psychology's counterpart to ERIC, the PsychLit database, listed over 16,500 articles and documents, while the Social Science Index indexed another 500 or so documents. Simple addition suggests that over 40,000 documents addressing the topic of motivation have been authored, and this number is probably a low estimate. So much has been written about this subject that the 40,001st document on motivation runs a high risk of adding very little to what we know about motivating others.

So why this book? I think that a relevant question, followed by clearly-articulated answers, might lend insight as to why this book and the accompanying volumes in "The School Leadership Library" should be important. The relevant question might be, "How much of what you learned in your administrator preparation program were (or are) you able to apply to the 'real-world' of practice?"

> . . . In educational administration, practitioners do not resort to the literature in the field because they know they will not find there current knowledge about how to solve the problems they are facing. (Silver, as quoted in Thomson, 1993, p. ix)

> New principal preparation programs must address the troublesome "clinical gap" that exists between classroom and practice, and between subject content and specific technique. To close this gap, a new starting point is required. Accordingly, the search for a knowledge and

> skills base should begin with the work of principals in contemporary schools. That work must first be defined and organized into identifiable, rational building blocks that are skill-rich and knowledge-rich. Next, the connections between knowledge and skills should be recognized in the many problems principals respond to and in the many tasks they initiate. (Thomson, 1993, pp. x-xi)

Therefore, the purpose of this volume is to take what we know about leader behavior in motivating others and tie it to the "real world" of school practice. The success of this volume will be judged by the extent to which this knowledge can serve to inform the practices of principals in motivating others.

WHAT MOTIVATION IS

Words have meaning. This is certainly no less true for the word "motivation." In fact, since motivation has been written about tens of thousands of times, you might expect more than one definition. Consider the following definitions:

> Motivation is made up of "all those inner striving conditions described as wishes, desires, drives, etc. . . . it is an inner state that activates or moves individuals." (Berelson and Steiner, as quoted in Owens, 1991, p. 102)

> . . . work motivation is defined as the complex forces, drives, needs, tension states, or other mechanisms that start and maintain work-related behaviors toward the achievement of personal goals. (Hoy and Miskel, 1991, p. 168)

> . . . *the initiation, intensity, and persistence of behavior.* (Geen, 1995, p. 2, emphasis in original)

> . . . the energization and direction of behavior. (Deci & Ryan, 1985, p. 3)

> Motivation is the level of effort an individual is willing to apply toward the achievement of a particular goal or motive. (Hersey and Blanchard, 1977, p. 16)

At least three themes can be gleaned from considering the above definitions. ***First,*** motivation involves the behavior of *indi-*

viduals. The idea that motivation is individually oriented has important implications for principals trying to motivate others. In fact, if motivation is individually oriented, principals really do *not* motivate others as much as principals *create conditions* in the workplace which enhance the ability of other individuals to motivate themselves. Aflie Kohn (in Brandt, 1995), in discussing student motivation, punctuates my point by noting, "It's remarkable how often educators use the word *motivation* when what they mean is *compliance.* Indeed, one of the fundamental myths in this area is that it is possible to motivate someone else" (p. 14, emphasis in original). ***Second,*** individual motivation is driven by something, whether it is goals, needs, or desires. Assuming this is true, principals who wish to be successful in creating conditions for motivation must be cognizant of the particular goals, needs, and desires which drive staff members to behave in certain ways. Whether these goals, needs, and desires are individually- or organizationally- oriented, or both, will be the subject of later discussion. ***Finally,*** motivation entails not only initiating, but also maintaining and directing behavior. Therefore, the principal's actions of creating conditions to enhance the motivation of others is not a "one-shot" effort. Certainly, extrinsic rewards which reinforce desired behaviors cannot be considered as a means for long-term maintenance and direction of behavior; principals' reward powers are not unlimited, nor are extrinsic resources. Principals who are effective "motivators" create other conditions which satisfy the needs of individuals within the school.

WHAT MOTIVATION IS NOT

In your professional and administrator preparation readings you undoubtedly have come across the concepts of motivation and job satisfaction. As often as not, these concepts have been used interchangeably, as if they meant the same thing. While there is a strong relationship between motivation and job satisfaction, I would like to argue that they are not the same thing (though I am certainly not the first to advance this argument). In the definitions cited, we noted that motivation connotes an inner state of values, desires, or needs which energize, direct, and maintain human behavior. If we focus for a moment on the idea that needs energize behavior, we can readily see the distinction between motivation and satisfaction. Needs which are fulfilled may satisfy but do not necessarily motivate; stated differently, needs which are satisfied do not motivate unless our behavior is necessary to satisfy those needs (Gunn, in Miskel & Ogawa, 1988). For example, each of us is paid a salary for what we do. In most cases this salary (though we're all underpaid!) is sufficient to satisfy such needs as food, shelter, clothing, and some level of security. This salary is little more than "a fair day's pay for a fair day's work"; further, this salary is going to be paid unless our work-related behavior is immoral, illegal, unethical, or not up to some minimum level of competence. However, this salary is not going to be a force which initiates, directs, and sustains our behavior; thus, payment of a salary satisfies a need but does not motivate.

On the other hand, we may have needs for promotion, recognition, belonging to a cohesive work group, or increased responsibility. To satisfy these needs, we might have to behave in certain ways such as taking graduate classes, becoming involved in district or campus level decision-making committees, becoming part of an instructional team, or taking on additional responsibilities (such as sponsoring extracurricular activities or assuming leadership responsibilities in local, state, or national professional organizations). In schools, a teacher may wish to become part of a multidisciplinary instructional team at the middle school level in order to satisfy an individual need for belonging as well as students' needs for a stable academic environment. To the extent that this team works cohesively to meet these ends, to that extent belonging to such a team satisfies this teacher's need for belonging. In this specific situation, the teacher had to fulfill an unmet need by behaving in a certain way. This need served as motivator in that the teacher's behavior was necessary to satisfy this need.

VIEWS OF PEOPLE AND MOTIVATION

Views of motivation are often shaped by the way we view other people. Those of us who have taken any administrator preparation classes are familiar with the X and Y Theories advanced by Douglas McGregor (1960). While these are sometimes mentioned as motivation theories, in reality these theories explain how we view other people. A person with a Theory X orientation views people as lazy, unmotivated, and hating work. A principal with this view of people would approach motivating others with the "carrot-and-stick" method; that is, providing extrinsic incentives to induce people to behave in certain ways. Conversely, a person with a Theory Y orientation assumes that others view work as naturally as play and derive a great deal of personal satisfaction from their work. A principal with this orientation would approach motivating teachers by creating conditions in the workplace which provide teachers with maximum opportunities for achievement, challenge, responsibility, autonomy, and advancement. These conditions and opportunities are not something that the principal can offer teachers as an exchange for behaving in a certain way; rather, these conditions are a requisite part of the work itself.

Thomas J. Sergiovanni (1992), in his book *Moral Leadership*, wonderfully expands upon these two orientations and their implications for motivating others to formulate three rules of motivation. The first two rules are similar to the views of people and motivation mentioned in the preceding paragraph. The first rule states that "What gets rewarded gets done" (p. 27) and represents the traditional view of motivating others. While acknowledging that this rule does have some validity in the workplace, Sergiovanni discusses several implications of this view of motivation. First, if this rule is valid, then its reverse also applies: "What does not get rewarded does not get done" (p. 24). Second, the person responsible for creating conditions for motivation in the workplace must be the monitor of rewards, thereby knowing which types of rewards satisfy which people, and must find some way to maintain a continuous flow of desired rewards to sustain behavior. Finally, those who receive the rewards in exchange for desired behavior become increasingly dependent on the rewards and the leader to provide the rewards; hence, this attachment serves to indenture people to rewards and actually discourages independence and autonomy. According to Sergiovanni, under the "What gets rewarded gets done" rule, people are motivated by extrinsic gain, and their involvement is calculated to receive rewards.

The second and an alternative motivation rule offered by

Sergiovanni (1992) states that "What is rewarding gets done" (p. 27). This view of motivating others aligns with a Theory Y view of people. A principal with such a view would structure the workplace to provide others with maximum opportunities for achievement, challenge, responsibility, autonomy, and advancement. In this type of workplace, then, work is accomplished without workers being indentured to rewards; moreover, the principal does not have to assume the role of reward monitor, and thus does not have to exercise close supervision over the work process. Under the "What is rewarding gets done" rule of motivation, people are motivated by intrinsic gain, and their involvement comes from within.

The third view of motivation is again an alternative to the first two and is based on Sergiovanni's (1992) concepts of professional and moral authority as sources or substitutes for leadership. Professional authority as the first source of leadership practice is defined as "craft knowledge and personal expertise" (p. 31). Moral authority as a second source of or substitute for leadership practice is based on "obligations and duties derived from widely shared values, ideas, and ideals" (p. 31). The rule of motivation based on professional and moral authority states that "What is good gets done" (p. 27). Good is defined as "What we believe in, and what we feel obligated to do because of a moral commitment. . . " (p. 27). This view of motivation is based on a shared and compelling vision and is driven by the culture of the organization, i.e., the shared beliefs, values, norms, or "the way we do things around here." Under the "What is good gets done" rule of motivation, people are motivated by a sense of duty or obligation, and their involvement is not calculated and is more than intrinsic. Indeed, their involvement is based on what is moral or good.

Although there is a need to provide *meaningful, work-related rewards* in schools, I believe that principals who create conditions which enable teachers to be self-motivated go well beyond the "What is rewarded gets done" rule to accomplish this creation. Thus, while I will discuss rewards as a necessary component of the principal's repertoire, I believe that it is important to focus more heavily on the effective strategies and practices to fulfill the second and third rules of motivation.

A LITTLE THEORY

Why a little theory? Another good question. As a very recent graduate student and school administrator, I often asked this question (sometimes I posed the question as "Why any theory?" or "What does this theory have to do with what is going on in my school?"). This book is supposed to help principals and prospective principals to *apply* the knowledge and skills from the 21 leadership domains recommended by the National Policy Board for Educational Administration (NPBEA). My intent is to provide practical strategies and tactics which can be applied to your daily professional work in the "real world." Therefore, a detailed discussion of a wide range of motivation theories is beyond the intent of this book.

All the same, theories are important if they are viewed as a way to help us describe, explain, and predict human behavior in schools; if they can help us "make sense" out of these behavioral complexities; and most importantly, if they provide us with one of many means to inform our practice (Sergiovanni, 1991). Theories are not prescriptive, providing a 'one best' approach to every situation which arises; rather, theories are informative, serving to enlighten our actions and to provide a basis for reflecting on these actions. Thus, if theories are of value, theories of motivation can help us lay the groundwork for a discussion of "how to" create the conditions for the self-motivation of others. As such, the theories to be examined on the following pages will be tied to the practical strategies of subsequent chapters.

CONTENT THEORIES OF MOTIVATION

As you know, there are many theories of motivation in the literature. In Thomson (1993), the team which developed the domain on Motivating Others drew upon two categories of motivation theories by which we can lay this groundwork. The first category of motivation theory is called content theory and focuses on the values and needs which motivate people; this category is best exemplified by two widely popular theories: Maslow's *Hierarchy of Needs Theory* (1954) and Herzberg's *Two-Factor Theory* (Herzberg, Mausner, and Snyderman, 1959). Both theories focus on the needs which people attempt to satisfy, and thus the needs which motivate, in the organization.

HIERARCHY OF NEEDS THEORY

In his *Hierarchy of Needs Theory*, Maslow (1954) posited that there are five categories of needs which people attempt to satisfy through their behavior. These categories are arranged in hierarchical order and are considered prepotent; that is, once a lower level need is satisfied, it no longer motivates a person and a more potent or higher level need takes its place. The categories of needs, arranged from lowest level to highest level, are listed below:

- *Basic physiological needs*—This category includes the needs for food, shelter, water, sex, sleep, and air.
- *Security and safety needs*—This category includes the needs for physical safety, order, structure, and financial security.
- *Social affiliation needs*—This category includes the needs for love, belonging to groups, friendship, and acceptance by others.
- *Esteem needs*—This category includes the needs for self-esteem or respect, recognition by peers, achievement, self-confidence, dignity, and appreciation.
- *Self-actualization needs*—This category includes the needs for maximum achievement of potential, self-expression, autonomy, self-direction, and creativity.

Lyman W. Porter (1961; see also Hoy & Miskel, 1991; Owens, 1991, 1995) revised Maslow's Hierarchy of Needs Theory to reflect what he thought to be the reality of most managers; namely, that most managers (and I assume this to be true for most school staff) are not motivated by basic physiological needs. As such, Porter's revision of Maslow's theory is probably more applicable to the professional setting. This assumption notwithstanding, Porter's Need Satisfaction Theory reflects Maslow's Hierarchy of Needs Theory in that the need categories are arranged in hierarchical and prepotent order as shown in Figure 1-1.

In addition to removing the category of physiological needs

FIGURE 1.1. NEEDS HIERARCHY THEORY BASED ON PORTER'S REVISION

SELF-ACTUALIZATION

Working at full potential
Feeling successful at work
Achieving significant goals

⇑

AUTONOMY

Control of work situation
Influence in organization
Decisional participation
Authority to use resources

⇑

SELF-ESTEEM

Feeling of self-respect
Titles, status symbols
Promotion, recognition, awards
Respect from others
Part of "inner circle"

⇑

AFFILIATION

Belonging to work group (formal & informal)
Peer acceptance
Friendships
Belonging to professional associations/unions

⇑

SECURITY

Salary, benefits, retirement plan
Union, seniority, tenure, due process
Acceptable personnel policies and procedures
Fair evaluations

From: Owens, R.G. *Organizational Behavior in Education* (5th ed.). Copyright © 1995 by Allyn and Bacon. Reprinted/adapted with permission.

from Maslow's hierarchy, Porter also removed the concept of autonomy from Maslow's self-actualization needs category and assigned autonomy to its own category. He inserted autonomy needs between self-esteem and self-actualization needs and defined autonomy as the degree to which one is in control of his/her work situation, has influence in the organization, participates in important decisions, and has authority to use organizational resources.

Porter's Need Satisfaction Model suggests that there are things that principals can do (and these are very general examples) to create conditions whereby individuals can satisfy unmet needs such that these unmet needs can serve as motivational forces. Under the security needs category, for example, principals can ensure that clear expectations for staff performance are established, that staff evaluations are fair and equitable, that working conditions free teachers to teach (such as reducing classroom interruptions and unnecessary paperwork, providing equitable class sizes and teaching loads, and intervening with students who pose serious discipline problems), and that teachers are provided formal and informal feedback. Under the affiliation needs category, principals can structure the organization of the school to reduce teacher isolation and provide opportunities for teachers to establish professional working relationships and personal friendships (e.g., Schools within schools, team teaching opportunities, and interaction with colleagues at professional meetings). Under the self-esteem needs category, principals can provide opportunities for promotion, recognition, and rewards; and can confer awards and titles (as insignificant as it might seem, professional business cards for all staff are really appreciated!). Under the autonomy needs category, principals can, for example, provide opportunities for teachers to participate in important decisions, confer greater authority in the procurement and use of organizational resources, and grant teachers greater control over their classrooms (such as encouraging teachers to teach "beyond the test"!). Finally, by organizing the school and providing teachers opportunities to fulfill the first four need levels, principals free teachers to work and achieve at their full potentials, thereby removing impediments to satisfying self-actualization needs.

TWO-FACTOR THEORY

The second content theory of motivation is Herzberg's *Two-Factor Theory* (Herzberg et al., 1959) (see Fig. 1.2). Unlike the Needs Hierarchy Theories, this theory suggests that motivation is two-dimensional, and that each dimension is comprised of distinct factors. According to Herzberg, the first set of factors (called *hygienes, maintenance factors*, or *dissatisfiers*), when not sufficiently present in the workplace, lead to job dissatisfaction. However, these hygiene factors, when sufficiently present in the organization, do not contribute to the job satisfaction of staff, but merely result in no dissatisfaction. These hygiene factors identified by Herzberg are *salary, benefits, interpersonal relations* with supervisors and peers, *type of supervision, administrative policies and attitudes, job security, and working conditions*. Thus, when these factors are sufficiently present in the workplace, teachers are not dissatisfied, but increasing these factors or the possibility of attaining these factors only means that job dissatisfaction is reduced, and not that motivation is increased.

The second set of factors in Herzberg's theory (called *motivators* or *satisfiers*), when sufficiently present in the workplace, contribute to the motivation of staff members and result in job satisfaction; when these factors are not sufficiently present, no satisfaction is the likely result. Herzberg identified these motivators as *achievement, advancement*, the *work itself, recognition, professional and personal growth*, and *responsibility*. Again, if these factors are not present in the school, satisfaction does not result, but job dissatisfaction does not follow.

A quick examination of Herzberg's Two-Factor Theory shows that the hygienes, which result in no dissatisfaction when sufficiently present in the workplace, are generally characteristics of the organization. Conversely, motivators, which can lead to satisfaction if sufficiently present in the workplace, are attributable to individuals and their perceptions of the degree to which these factors are present in the organization (Owens, 1991). This examination suggests at least a couple of implications for principals who wish to create conditions for teachers to motivate themselves. ***First***, the principal's ability to exercise direct influence over some of the hygiene factors is rather limited. For example, in most schools direct control over salaries

FIGURE 1.2. HERZBERG'S TWO-FACTOR THEORY OF MOTIVATION

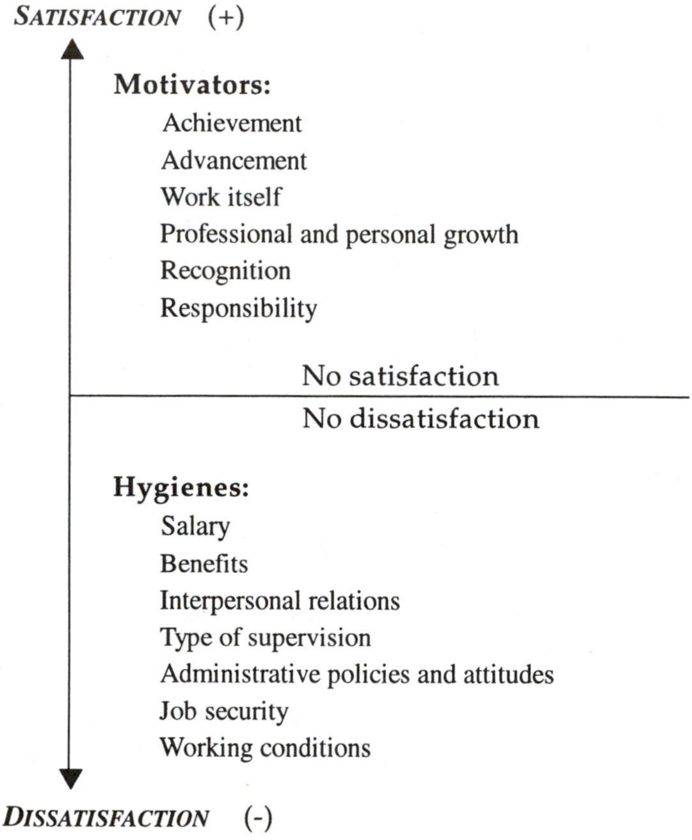

and benefits is vested in the central administration and the school board. To the extent that job security is created by contractual obligations between the school district and teachers, to a similar extent job security is beyond the principal's direct control. Moreover, many administrative policies and attitudes emanate from beyond the campus level and are as well beyond the principal's direct control. Although the principal certainly has a greater level of influence over type of supervision, interpersonal relations (see Chapter 7), and working conditions (such as reducing interruptions during the school day, and maintaining effective student discipline procedures), Herzberg advocates that a sufficient presence of these factors in the workplace only reduces job dissatisfaction.

The ***second*** implication for principals relates to the degree of influence that the principal has over the motivators. It certainly seems evident that principals can have a greater influence over the degree to which individually-oriented motivational factors are present in the school. For example, principals can certainly provide opportunities for teachers to experience professional and personal growth (such as teacher-led campus professional development, release time and financial support to attend professional meetings), for responsibility and advancement (such as appointment to meaningful campus or district level committees, department chairships, interdisciplinary team leaders, attendance and disciplinary appeals committees, etc.), and for recognition of achievement (see Chapter 6). In sum, while hygiene factors are "tangible" factors which can result in dissatisfaction if reduced, the motivators are those "intangible" factors which can lead to personal and professional satisfaction if principals design the workplace so that opportunities to experience these factors are plentiful.

When we align Porter's and Herzberg's theories of motivation, we can identify themes common to each and strengthen our understanding of the needs that motivate others (Owens, 1991) (see Fig. 1.3). This alignment indicates that security and affiliation needs, which are organizationally oriented, are very similar to hygiene factors. Moreover, self-esteem, autonomy, and self-actualization needs, which are individually oriented, can be thought of as very similar to the motivation factors. The implication is clear: Principals who wish to create conditions whereby staff can motivate themselves will be successful only if they can organize the workplace so that teachers have real and meaningful opportunities to satisfy these higher-order needs.

FIGURE 1.3. COMPARING PORTER'S NEED HIERARCHY THEORY AND HERZBERG'S TWO-FACTOR THEORY

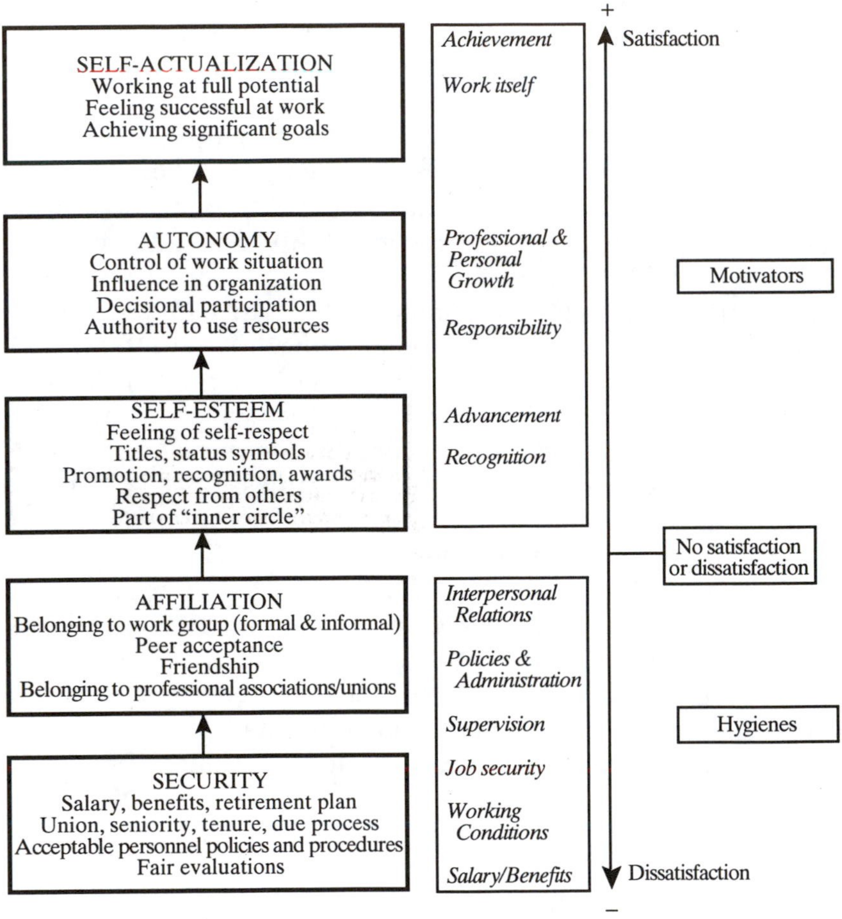

PROCESS THEORIES OF MOTIVATION

The second category of motivation theory discussed in Thomson (1993), called process theories of motivation, emphasizes how human behavior is initiated, sustained, and extinguished. This category is best exemplified by the Expectancy Model of Motivation (see Fig. 1.4) based on the work of Victor Vroom (1964) and others (Daft, 1988; Hoy & Miskel, 1991; Thomson, 1993).

According to this model of motivation, a person is motivated to put forth an effort to attain a certain level of performance. This motivation is influenced by *expectancy*, or the probability that a given effort will lead to a desired level of performance. In addition, a person's motivation is influenced by *instrumentality*, or the probability that a given level of performance will result in an outcome. These outcomes could be rewards, incentives, recognition, achievement of goals, etc. Finally, a person's motivation is influenced by the *valence*, or the desirability or value that is assigned to this outcome.

For example, suppose that a middle school principal wishes to reduce the number of student discipline referrals for the upcoming school year. As part of this project, her site-based decision-making team selects a study team of two teachers and one assistant principal to visit other middle school campuses which have been successful in reducing the number of discipline referrals, to gather the "best practices" from each of these schools, and to provide a full day session of staff development at the beginning of the new school year. The motivation, and thus the effort, of this team is no doubt influenced by *expectancy*; accordingly, if the team believes that its efforts have a good chance to improve the performance of the entire staff in classroom management, then the team is likely to be motivated to put forth a desirable effort. The team's motivation to fulfill its responsibilities is further influenced by *instrumentality*; thus, if the team believes that improved performance by the staff in classroom management is likely to lead to improved student behavior, its motivation will increase. Finally, the level of motivation of the team will depend on *valence*, or the value that the team places on improved student behavior as well as other desired individual outcomes. If the team attaches a high degree of value

FIGURE 1.4. EXPECTANCY MODEL OF MOTIVATION

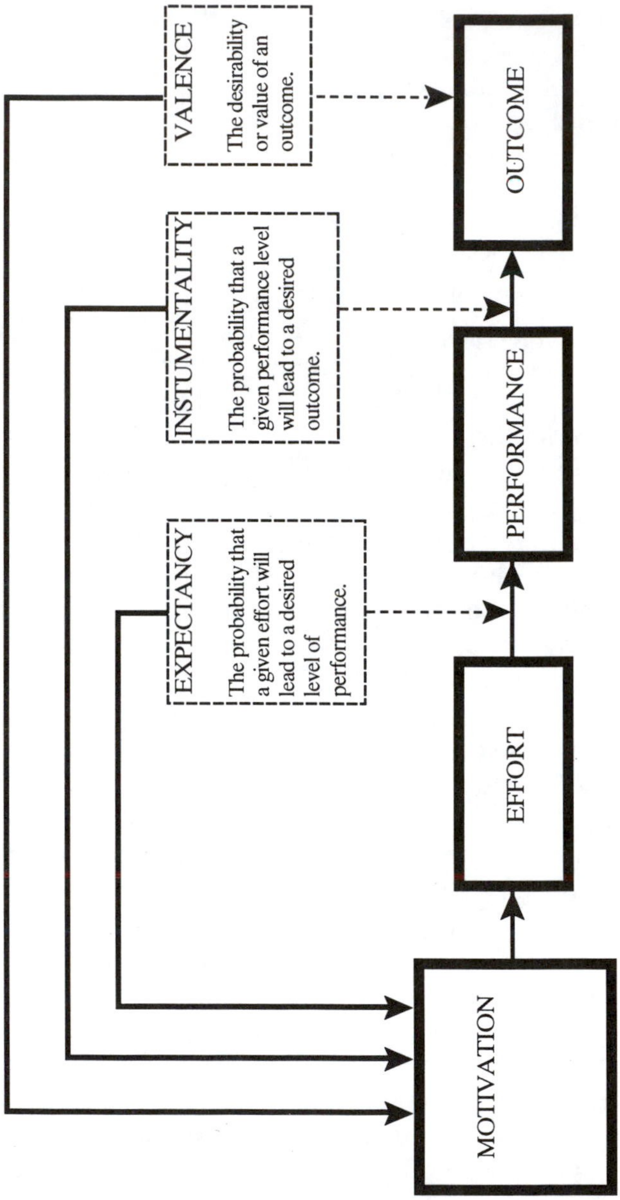

to improved student behavior as well as desired individual outcomes (e.g., public recognition at a school board meeting and/or an opportunity to present the improved discipline program at professional meetings), the team's motivation to effectively complete its assignment is very likely to be high.

This model of motivation assumes that persons in organizations make conscious choices about their behavior by thinking about and anticipating future events (Hoy & Miskel, 1996). Even so, there are things that the principal could do in the above example to enhance the expectancy and instrumentality probabilities and the valence of outcomes. To influence motivation by strengthening the probability that the team's efforts will lead to improved performance (*expectancy*), she can set and communicate her expectations for student behavior to the instructional staff, express to the staff her confidence that student behavior will improve, involve instructional staff in revising student behavior expectations and organizational arrangements, secure time and resources for both the team and other instructional staff to gather additional information, assist individual teachers with goal setting for the next year, and attend staff development seminars with teachers. To influence motivation by strengthening the probability that improved staff performance will result in desired work outcomes (*instrumentality*), the principal can determine the valued outcomes of the study team and individual teachers, recognize the study team and teachers for bringing about improvements in student behavior, provide teachers with information showing how improved student behavior relates to student achievement, support teachers in student discipline matters, and provide tangible and intangible rewards for improving student behavior.

I hope these motivation theories serve to illustrate some of the things principals can do to create conditions whereby staff can be motivated. Before we really get into the "practical," I would like to elaborate on: (1) A general model of job design which informs how principals can create these conditions, and (2) an assessment which principals can use to gauge teachers' perceptions of these characteristics in the school setting.

CREATING CONDITIONS

The Job Characteristics Model (JCM) of Work Motivation (Fig. 1.5) is a model of job design which has important implications for principals who wish to create conditions whereby teachers experience high intrinsic work motivation. Developed by J. Richard Hackman and Greg M. Oldham (1976), this model of motivation is widely cited in the literature and is a central focus of the chapter on "Motivating Others" in Thomson (1993). Moreover, this model integrates Maslow-Porter's *Needs Hierarchy Theory*, Herzberg's *Two-Factor Theory*, and *Expectancy Theory* into a model of job design (Hoy & Miskel, 1991).

As the model suggests, there are three psychological states which are necessary for people to have if they are to experience, among other important personal and work outcomes, high intrinsic motivation. These three states and their definitions are cited below (see Hackman & Oldham, 1976; Hoy & Miskel, 1996):

- *Experienced/Felt Meaningfulness of the Work*: The degree to which a person perceives and experiences his/her work as worthy, valuable, and important.
- *Experienced/Felt Responsibility for Work Outcomes*: The degree to which a person perceives and experiences personal accountability and responsibility for the results of his/her work.
- *Knowledge of Work Results*: The degree to which a person continuously knows and understands how effectively he/she is performing the job.

The extent to which individuals in the organization experience these three critical psychological states is influenced by the presence of certain core job characteristics in each individual's work activities. The three job characteristics which influence experienced/felt meaningfulness of the work are skill variety, task identity, and task significance. Each is defined below:

- *Skill variety*: The degree to which a job requires a variety of activities, and thus requires a person to draw on a wide array of skills and talents to perform the job.
- *Task identity*: The degree to which a job requires a person to complete a "whole" piece of work (e.g., assembling a

bicycle) rather than completing only a portion of a task (e.g., attaching kickstands to bicycles).

- *Task significance*: The degree to which a job has a substantial impact on the lives of other people, either inside or outside the organization.

Experienced/felt responsibility for work outcomes is influenced by the core job characteristic of *autonomy*, defined as the degree to which a person has freedom, discretion, and independence to schedule and carry out the work. Knowledge of work results is influenced by the core job characteristic of *feedback*, or the degree to which the work activities continuously inform a person how effectively he/she is performing the job.

As the model implies, if a person's job is characterized by a high degree of the core job characteristics, he/she is more likely to experience the three critical psychological states and thus is likely to possess a higher degree of intrinsic motivation. However, the model also suggests that the relationships between the core job characteristics, critical psychological states, and personal and work outcomes are likely to be stronger if a person possesses a high need for growth (personal development), accomplishment, and learning (Hackman & Oldham, 1976); has the requisite knowledge and skills to perform the job; and is satisfied with work conditions (similar to Herzberg's hygienes) (Hoy & Miskel, 1996). By application, teachers with little or no need for growth and personal development are less likely to be motivated even if they possess requisite knowledge and skills and are satisfied with work conditions. These individuals are the few teachers in the building who, after sincere yet unsuccessful attempts by the principal to remediate, must be terminated from employment.

FIGURE 1.5. JOB CHARACTERISTICS OF WORK MOTIVATION

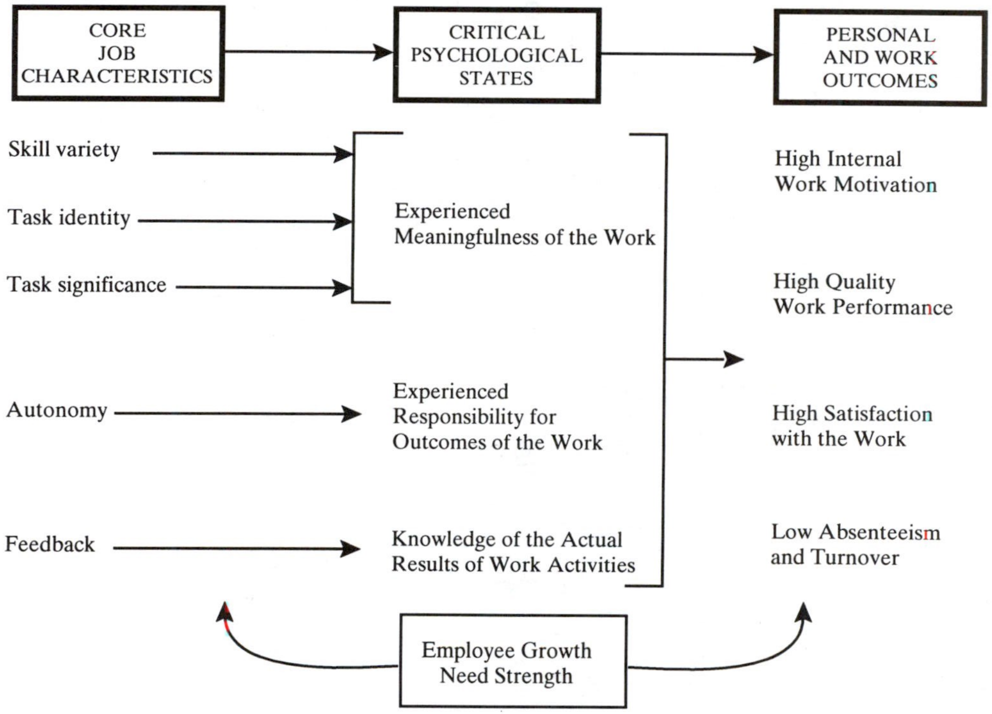

From: Hackman, J.R., & Oldham, G.R. (1976). Motivation through the design of work: Test of a theory. *Organizational Behavior and Human Performance, 16*, 250-279. Copyright © 1976 by Academic Press. Reprinted with permission of Academic Press and authors.

By application to our settings, the critical psychological states which lead to intrinsic motivation are internal to persons and are thus not subject to direct manipulation by the principal (nor should they be!). However, since these states are influenced largely by the five core job characteristics, it becomes apparent that the principal has a great deal of influence on the degree to which these characteristics are present in the school. As such, the principal can create conditions or set the stage whereby these characteristics are sufficiently present for staff to experience the critical psychological states and thus become intrinsically self-motivated. It is around these job characteristics and their applications that the rest of this volume is organized.

WHERE DO WE GO FROM HERE?

To answer simply, the pages which follow are designed to make real much of what we have discussed in this first chapter on setting the stage. By making it this far, I trust you have gained a conceptual understanding of some of the conditions that must be present in schools that can lead to teachers' intrinsic self-motivation and, as importantly, conditions that can lead to an unmotivated professional staff.

I believe that effective principals are cognizant of and want to know the perceptions of their staffs regarding job conditions that can serve to motivate or discourage. Thus, as a beginning of the "practical" side of motivating others, I have included in Figure 1.6, a job conditions questionnaire and an explanation of its use. The format and about one-half of the items are adapted from Sergiovanni (1991, 1995, *The Principalship: A Reflective Practice Perspective*); the other one-half of the items I wrote, to attempt to assess other job characteristics principals can influence to improve teachers' critical psychological states. Thereby setting the stage for teachers' intrinsic motivation. You can use this questionnaire to assess teachers' perceptions of these conditions in your school; indeed, you might even venture to complete this questionnaire to predict teachers' perceptions. If your assessment of these job conditions is more favorable than that of your teachers, there are probably motivation strategies you can draw upon to narrow these gaps and truly "set the stage" for individual intrinsic motivation.

ACTION PLAN

For each of the first six chapters, I have suggested an action plan that you might use to immediately apply some of the practical strategies discussed in each chapter. By no means should you consider these suggestions to be exhaustive; indeed, the greatest benefit of these action plans will come from the additional ideas that you generate from your reading and reflecting. As such, I encourage you to add other strategies to each Action Plan.

- Using the questionnaire in Figure 1.6, assess your faculty's perceptions of the job conditions in your building and compare them to your prediction of teacher responses. Take all steps necessary to ensure the anonymity of teacher responses. Use the comparisons to focus on job conditions that need immediate and long-term improvement.
- Consider the example provided on pages 17 and 18 describing how a middle school principal's attempts to reduce the number of discipline referrals in her school was traced in terms of the Expectancy Model of Motivation. Apply the same model to attempts you have made in the past to work through other people to make similar and needed changes in your school. Also consider using the model to propose activities that you could initiate to effect some changes you would like to implement.
- Meet with a group of peers who have also worked through the plan above. Compare and contrast your separate applications of this model. Does the model inform past and future behavior?

SUGGESTED READINGS

The following suggested readings will supplement and enhance the content in each of the first six chapters. Where applicable, especially pertinent sections of the readings are highlighted.

Hoy, W.K., & Miskel, C.G. (1991). *Educational administration: Theory, research, practice* (4th ed.). New York: McGraw-Hill.

(See especially Chapter 7 titled "Work Motivation in Schools" for an excellent overview of work motivation theories).

Thomson, S.D. (Ed.) (1993). *Principals for our changing schools.* Fairfax, VA: National Policy Board for Educational Administration. (See especially Chapter 14 titled "Motivating Others" for a brief and excellent overview of content and process theories of motivation and the general application of these theories to principals' work).

FIGURE 1.6. JOB CONDITIONS QUESTIONNAIRE

(From Sergiovanni, T.J. *The Principalship: A Reflective Practice Perspective* (3rd ed.). Copyright © 1995 by Allyn and Bacon. Reprinted/adapted with permission. Adapted from a more general questionnaire developed by Pfeiffer, J.W., & Goodstein, L.D. (1984), *The 1984 Annual: Developing Human Resources.* San Diego, CA: Pfeiffer & Company.)

DIRECTIONS: Please respond to the following questions to objectively describe the characteristics of your job and the activities of colleagues and supervisors. These questions are not designed to assess your like or dislike for your job, but rather are designed to assess as objectively as possible your objective perceptions of the following job conditions. For each question, please circle the appropriate response.

SA (Strongly agree), A (Agree), D (Disagree), SD (Strongly disagree)

1. Teachers in my school make some decisions about their work, but most decisions must be referred to teachers' supervisors or are influenced by policy, curriculum, or testing requirements. SA A D SD
2. Teachers in my school have clear expectations for their performance and participate in setting these expectations. SA A D SD
3. Teachers in my school are required to cover a specific amount of material each week. SA A D SD
4. Teachers in my school perform repetitive tasks. SA A D SD
5. My principal regularly communicates to teachers that their work is meaningful. SA A D SD
6. Teachers in my position have extensive control over their work activities. SA A D SD

7. My principal regularly recognizes teachers for a job well done. SA A D SD
8. Teachers in my school are encouraged to become involved in student activities. SA A D SD
9. Teachers in my school are required to follow certain procedures in doing their work that they would not follow if they had the choice. SA A D SD
10. Teachers in my job often work alone on their teaching with little or no contact with colleagues. SA A D SD
11. Teachers in my school must refer teaching problems to their supervisor before taking action. SA A D SD
12. Teachers in my job are regularly provided with formal and informal performance-related feedback. SA A D SD
13. My work involves completing "whole" tasks. SA A D SD
14. My principal provides opportunities for teachers to update their skills. SA A D SD
15. My work requires extensive contact with other teachers. SA A D SD
16. My principal regularly solicits and considers teachers' input on matters affecting teachers' work. SA A D SD
17. Teachers in my position are evaluated according to clear, agreed-upon expectations. SA A D SD
18. Teachers in my building have considerable input into the type of classes that they teach. SA A D SD
19. My work requires me to learn new methods and skills in order to keep pace with changes and new developments. SA A D SD
20. Teachers in my school believe their work is important. SA A D SD
21. Teachers in my position can make their own decisions without checking with anyone else or without consulting approved curricular and instructional requirements. SA A D SD
22. My job provides me with knowledge of the effectiveness of my performance. SA A D SD

23. Teachers in my building perform fragmented and unrelated tasks. SA A D SD
24. Teachers in my position perform similar tasks each day. SA A D SD
25. Teachers in my position have opportunities to learn about the teaching that occurs at other grade levels and in other departments. SA A D SD

Scoring Instructions: For each item, transfer the responses for each of the 25 questions to the grid below by circling the number below the appropriate response. For example, if you circled "A" for item 1, circle "2" in the box headed "Ques. 1." After transferring the responses for each of the 25 items, add the numbers for each of the columns and place the total in the empty box below each column. The higher the score for each column, the more favorable are the job conditions that influence the critical psychological states and thus the potential for teachers' self-motivation.

Ques. 1 SA A D SD 1 2 3 4	Ques. 2 SA A D SD 4 3 2 1	Ques. 3 SA A D SD 1 2 3 4	Ques. 4 SA A D SD 1 2 3 4	Ques. 5 SA A D SD 4 3 2 1
Ques. 6 SA A D SD 4 3 2 1	Ques. 7 SA A D SD 4 3 2 1	Ques. 8 SA A D SD 4 3 2 1	Ques. 9 SA A D SD 1 2 3 4	Ques. 10 SA A D SD 1 2 3 4
Ques. 11 SA A D SD 1 2 3 4	Ques. 12 SA A D SD 4 3 2 1	Ques. 13 SA A D SD 4 3 2 1	Ques. 14 SA A D SD 4 3 2 1	Ques. 15 SA A D SD 4 3 2 1
Ques. 16 SA A D SD 4 3 2 1	Ques. 17 SA A D SD 4 3 2 1	Ques. 18 SA A D SD 4 3 2 1	Ques. 19 SA A D SD 4 3 2 1	Ques. 20 SA A D SD 4 3 2 1
Ques. 21 SA A D SD 4 3 2 1	Ques. 22 SA A D SD 4 3 2 1	Ques. 23 SA A D SD 1 2 3 4	Ques. 24 SA A D SD 1 2 3 4	Ques. 25 SA A D SD 4 3 2 1
Autonomy	Feedback	Task Identity	Skill Variety	Task Significance

Score interpretation for each column:

5–10	Unfavorable job conditions
11–15	Moderately favorable job conditions
16–20	Highly favorable job conditions

2

FOSTERING TEAMWORK, COLLEGIALITY, AND PARTICIPATION

"We must all hang together or we will hang separately"
Benjamin Franklin

While Ben Franklin was not referring to schooling or education in this comment, I think that his wise words can be applied to schools today. I hardly need to repeat that while our schools continue to bear criticism (some of it justified, some of it not), our schools are still expected to educate all children and remedy society's ills. The educational landscape is cluttered with calls for reform, restructuring, charter schools, and even privatization. Regardless of what schools look like five, ten, or fifty years from now, one feature that I think (and hope) will remain is school campuses with teachers teaching kids, live and in color. And as long as teachers are teaching kids, someone is going to be held ultimately responsible for the success or failure of the students in that school. It really does not matter if the accountable person is the principal, headmaster/headmistress, dean, or lead teacher; the buck is going to stop somewhere. And when that buck stops, the success of the students and the school will be determined largely by the ability of the school to function as a team in pursuit of accomplishing the mission of student success. Therefore, the leader of the school (whom we still refer to as the principal) must organize and nurture this team so that collegiality and participation are the norm, teacher motivation is the by-product, and student success is the result.

In Chapter 1, we noted that principals do not "motivate others"; rather, principals influence and even create the job conditions that can result in teachers' intrinsic motivation. Please recall two of the critical psychological states which are necessary for teachers to experience intrinsic motivation:

- *Experienced/felt meaningfulness of the work,* which was defined as the degree to which a person perceives and experiences his/her work as worthy, valuable, and important; and
- *Experienced/felt responsibility for work outcomes,* which was defined as the degree to which a person perceives and experiences personal accountability and responsibility for the results of his/her work.

In general, principals create conditions for teachers to experience and feel that their work is meaningful by creating teams, encouraging collegiality, removing barriers to teachers' classroom isolation, and designing the job so that teachers use a variety of skills and perform complete tasks. By doing so, principals create conditions which increase the likelihood that teachers' work has substantial influence on the lives of others. Principals also create conditions for teachers to experience and feel responsibility for work outcomes by involving them in decisions which affect their daily work and by providing autonomy for them to exercise professional judgment over their daily work. In this chapter we will discuss strategies that principals can use to foster teamwork, collegiality, and participation so that school staff can "hang together" and avoid "hanging separately."

TEAMWORK AND COLLEGIALITY

I have always believed in organized athletics as a way to become part of and function as a team. My first experience in Little League baseball comes directly to mind. My dad, Doug Thompson, was our coach. The rosters came out at the beginning of the summer; when they came out and I looked at the roster, I told my dad, "there's no way we'll win even one game." I don't remember my dad saying much to my comment, except maybe "let's practice and wait and see." To make a long story short, the summer came and went and the Cambridge "Indians" won the Little League championship with an undefeated record. Without question, I learned that teams with less talent can (and often do) overtake teams with superior talent. Even more importantly, I learned three additional lessons:

- When an organization functions as a team, the whole truly becomes greater than the sum of its parts.
- As part of the team, each person can develop collegial relationships with teammates.
- Leadership matters.

However, just like the baseball coach, the school principal doesn't "make the plays"; the principal (coach) creates the conditions (teamwork) whereby the staff (players) make the plays. Thus, the success of the leader in creating the conditions of teamwork determines the degree to which the players feel and function as part of a team. The extent to which the players feel and function as part of a team results in the intrinsic motivation necessary to "make the plays."

A successful school should look an awful lot like a baseball team. On a baseball team, players experience and feel that their work is meaningful in three ways. ***First,*** baseball players are required to utilize a *wide variety of skills*. For example, they must be able to catch, hit, throw, run, bunt, and think. Players who possess each of these physical skills but consistently "throw behind the runner" (i.e., throw the ball to second base while the base runner is heading to third) hurt the team and usually find work on the bench or elsewhere. In schools, teachers must be competent in subject matter, instructional methodologies, technology, classroom management, curricular innovations, identifying students who aren't "getting it," remediation, testing, and even counseling. A teacher who possesses exceptional subject matter knowledge but cannot manage students or identify students with learning difficulties slows the team's progress. ***Second,*** baseball players are required to *complete whole tasks* in order for the team to be successful. Although a play (task) in baseball is initiated by the pitcher, the other eight players on the field perform a whole task on each play. All players are required to know the number of outs and the count, to be positioned in the right place on the field, to know where they will throw the ball if it is hit to them, to know the tendencies of the hitters and runners, and to know the players whom they are supposed to back up. Each play requires each player to complete a whole task. Likewise, staff members on a successful school team experience this task identity (although this is not always the case) by having jobs structured so that they are responsible for the entire task of educating students. Teachers must be cognizant of students' prior academic performance, current academic performance in all subject areas, external factors which might impede students' ability to learn, behavioral tendencies, instructional strategies which will benefit students, and so on. ***Third,*** baseball teams are structured for maximum task significance in that each player's action has a substantial impact on the lives or actions of others on the team. For example, when a batter misses the third base coach's sign to swing away to protect the runner stealing second base, more often than not the runner will be thrown out. An error by the shortstop may cause a run to score and a big inning to continue. Whether we acknowledge it or not, the same is true for the school team. Consider these statements for a moment:

- The success (or failure) of students in Algebra I depends on the success (or failure) of students in seventh grade math.
- The success of students in chemistry depends on the success of students in algebra.
- The success of students in third grade reading depends on the success of students in first grade reading.
- The success of students in history depends on the success of students in language arts.
- The success of students in elementary school vocal music depends on the success of students in reading.
- The success of teachers in classroom management depends on the success of principals in supporting teachers.
- The ability of principals to "get out of the office" and be leaders of instruction depends on the ability of

teachers to effectively manage classrooms.

The list goes on. Thus, the team approach is already in place in schools, whether we like it or not. Therefore, the principal's responsibility is to structure, lead, and coach this team so that it functions like a team in pursuit of shared goals, and does not resemble a bunch of people running in different directions.

A natural by-product of being part of a successful team is the collegiality that teamwork fosters. Sergiovanni (1991, p. 138) defines collegiality as "the existence of high levels of collaboration among teachers and between teachers and principal and is characterized by mutual respect, *shared work values*, cooperation, and specific conversations about teaching and learning" (emphasis in original). Moreover, collegiality transcends congeniality (Sergiovanni, 1992), which is characterized by friendly relationships, trust, loyalty, and cohesiveness. Congeniality can help establish collegiality; but shared goals, shared beliefs, and mutual respect (i.e., confidence of all parties in the abilities and motivations of others) set collegiality apart from congeniality. If you think back to when you were part of a successful team, what was the nature of the relationships with your teammates? In most situations, I'll bet that not only did you function successfully as a team, but you probably became colleagues in pursuit of a common purpose; developed mutual respect for teammates' commitment, talent, and motivation; and perhaps formed long-lasting friendships. We have already noted that individuals have needs for affiliation, peer acceptance, collegiality, and friendship; clearly, the school team or teams can fulfill these needs. We logically must turn, then, to things that principals can do to foster this teamwork and collegiality.

FOSTERING TEAMWORK AND COLLEGIALITY

A school is a team, whether it functions as one or not. The teaching/learning process is the major activity in any school. Yet, teaching remains one of the most isolated jobs in any profession. Consider the words of Ann Lieberman and Lynne Miller (1984, p. 11):

> For most teachers in most schools, teaching is indeed a lonely enterprise. With so many people en-

> gaged in so common a mission in so compact a space and time, it is perhaps the greatest irony—and the greatest tragedy of teaching—that so much is carried on in self-imposed and professionally sanctioned isolation.

Does your school "look" like this? Does it have to "look" like this?

Where a team and collegial environment does not exist, the principal is the logical person to initiate the movement toward such an environment (assuming that the principal is committed to such a structure). The principal can create these conditions by considering and implementing many of the following strategies:

- **Continually articulate a vision for excellence** in which each staff member shares and becomes an integral part. All successful teams have a shared focus, mission, or goal which becomes their "rallying" point. Certainly, a shared vision for and common commitment to educational excellence for all students is something around which an entire staff can and should rally.
- **Continually articulate your confidence in team members** to realize this vision for excellence while **assessing your staff's readiness** for teamwork and collegiality.
- Around this vision, the principal must **set, communicate, and model clear expectations** for teamwork and collegiality. These expectations include a commitment to do the work necessary to accomplish the vision.
- As part of setting, communicating, and modeling clear expectations, the principal **organizes the school** to remove physical barriers to teamwork. Principals who "talk the talk" and then place the second grade team in the four corners of the building are not removing physical barriers.
- To the extent possible, **construct the master schedule** so that team members have common meeting periods.
- **Provide formal opportunities** and the **time** for team activities.
- **Institute informal opportunities** for team activities.

- Be flexible and **convene ad hoc teams** as campus issues need to be addressed and resolved.
- **Be available and participate**! This might be the principal's most important modeling behavior. Nothing disgusts teachers more quickly than when the "teamwork" principal doesn't show to a team activity.
- **Carefully listen to and consider** what the team thinks!
- **Provide recognition and rewards** for team members.

Ken McKinney, former principal of Westfield High School in the Spring (Texas) Independent School District in suburban north Houston, comes directly to mind when I think about a principal who not only espoused, but lived the team concept. I was quickly introduced to teaming when I had my first interview for assistant principal with the eight person AT (administrative team). By the time the first day of classes started in August 1991 (after only four weeks on the job), I had been completely socialized into a working, breathing, team concept. I quickly learned about the AT, the IT (instructional team), the CT (counseling team), the SAT (student assistance team), the GLT (grade level team) and other teams which were comprised of academic department members, subject area teachers, and so on. Unlike other schools which claimed to espouse the team concept, under the leadership of Ken McKinney, the team concept was part of the Westfield High School culture (as well as part of the culture of Spring ISD). This team concept fostered the collegiality alluded to by Sergiovanni (1992) in that the collegiality was based on shared work values (providing the best possible opportunity for student academic excellence) and mutual respect (confidence in the intentions and abilities of team members).

As I reflect upon my time as an assistant principal at Westfield High School, the culture of the school and the district, and the leadership provided by Ken McKinney (as well as by superintendent Gordon Anderson and assistant superintendent Rob Smith), I am now able to see how Ken "created the conditions" for teamwork and collegiality among the staff by:

- **Continually articulating the Westfield vision** for student academic excellence and providing students with every opportunity to excel academically. This vision also came from the district level and was exemplified by the four cornerstones of Spring ISD: "Instruction, Love, Discipline, Authority."

- **Continually articulating his confidence in the Westfield staff** to realize this vision for excellence. Ken never missed an opportunity to publicly tell the staff how much he believed in their ability to educate students or to publicly tell others how much confidence he placed in the school staff.
- **Setting, communicating, and modeling clear expectations** for teamwork and collegiality. There was absolutely no question that teamwork and collegiality were the norms at Westfield High School. For example, my first major task as a member of the ninth grade team (one of at least three teams I found myself a part of immediately) was to help organize our annual freshman student and parent orientation. Although my colleague and the other ninth grade assistant principal, Devery Parker, and I were responsible for the success of the orientation, it was the ninth grade team which had to pull off the entire happening. Our ninth grade team consisted of us, both ninth grade counselors, and all teachers who taught predominantly ninth grade subjects. In addition, each of the other members of the AT (administrative team) participated in speaking to parents. To help make this event successful, we also drew upon students to speak to the incoming freshmen, to speak to parents of freshmen, to take freshmen students on tours of the building, and to serve refreshments to and to socialize with the incoming students. Obviously, we wanted freshmen to be ready for the first day of class in the 2,750 student school; equally obvious was the fact that successfully conducting this event without the support of each team member would have been impossible. Ken McKinney set, communicated, and modeled his expectations for teamwork and collegiality and to do "whatever it took" to make it work.

- **Organizing the school** to remove as many possible barriers to teamwork. Ken and his right-hand associate principal Carm Castoria organized the building to make sure that each academic department was housed together, with classrooms in immediate proximity and a centralized workroom to make sure that teachers in each academic department could and had to talk to each other. Moreover, there was an assistant principal in each corner of the building (as opposed to centrally located) so that we could talk to teachers on a moment's notice and between each class period. Finally, each academic department was organized into teams according to subject area (for example, the English department had four teams comprised of English I, II, III, and IV teachers, respectively) with a team leader heading each team. Not only did this physical organization provide for quick communication, but it also provided the opportunities for many **rich, informal interactions** about teaching and learning.
- **Constructing the master schedule** so that team members have opportunities to interact. Although this is probably more difficult in a large school, Ken and his other right-hand associate principal, Jeannie Heiskell, were at least able to construct this schedule so that each department had common lunch periods and activity/study periods. To the extent possible, common planning periods for subject level or interdisciplinary team members is ideal.
- **Providing formal opportunities** and the **time** for team activities. Ken was a master at this. The AT (administrative team) met every Monday immediately after school (The expectation that our "second" day began at 2:45 p.m. was very clear at the outset). The IT (instructional team) met every Thursday morning during first period (since all academic department chairs were released from first period teaching obligations). Department meetings were held Friday mornings before first period (since teachers had no before or after school duties). Academic team meetings were held as needed.

Grade level team meetings were held at least once per 6-week grading period immediately after school. I could go on and on. Suffice it to say that Ken's ability to organize the school, the school day, and to remove teachers from non-instructional duties provided ample formal opportunities and time for team activities. In addition to campus level teams, many of the teaching staff at Westfield were involved in district level teams for which formal opportunities, released time, compensation, and recognition were provided.

- **Instituting informal opportunities** for team activities. The nature of the team concept as it was (and is) instituted at Westfield High School provided ample opportunities. It seemed commonplace for impromptu meetings of various teams to occur. Many of the administrative team's best meetings and decisions occurred during dining room (there was no lunch room at Westfield!) duty. Finally, many teams instituted their own informal, and even social, team activities.
- **Convening ad hoc teams** as issues needed to be addressed. For example, to respond to teachers' concerns about increasing student tardiness, Ken convened a team of teachers and administrators to rework the student tardy policy. In addition, I found myself on at least one ad hoc campus or district committee yearly (e.g., community involvement, drug-free schools, research on effects of block scheduling).
- **Being available and participating in team activities**. As principal, Ken was part of the administrative, instructional, and counseling teams; moreover, he kept abreast of grade level team activities. Finally, he initiated and instituted social activities for the "school team" such as the beginning of the year luncheon, Thanksgiving dinner, Christmas breakfast, and the annual fish fry. Keep in mind that these activities are important to the entire staff!
- **Carefully listening to and considering** what the team thinks. In the team concept at Westfield, Ken listened carefully and fully considered the implications of all

decision alternatives. In nearly all cases team agreed upon decisions were implemented.

- **Providing recognition and rewards** for team members. I have already noted how teacher non-instructional duties (bus, hallway) were virtually non-existent at Westfield and how time and opportunities were provided for formal and informal team activities. Teachers at Westfield were provided released time for professional development activities, district team leader training, a stipend for serving as a team leader, and just plain old sincere "well dones" for participating in and leading team activities.

These teamwork and collegiality strategies and practices certainly do not represent all of those available to the building principal. Moreover, teamwork and collegiality alone are not a panacea that will remedy all teacher motivation concerns. Indeed, other conditions (to be discussed throughout this book) must be in place to complement teamwork and collegiality as a condition for teacher motivation. Yet, these strategies and practices can provide the foundation for successfully implementing a team approach in your building.

Does teaming work? Yes. Can collegiality result? Yes. In the three years that I was at Westfield High School verbal and quantitative SAT scores rose nearly 75 points, with no decrease in the number of students taking the test (I am not suggesting that my presence had anything to do with the increase in SAT scores!). Was everything perfect at Westfield High School? By no means! But, as problems arose, we knew that these problems were not insurmountable because of the "will do" attitude of teammates coupled with the collegiality built on a deep and shared commitment to academic excellence and respect for the talents, abilities, and judgments of the staff. Do leaders matter? Without question!

PARTICIPATION IN DECISION-MAKING

Although I believe that participation (particularly in decision-making) cannot and should not be separated from teamwork and collegiality, participation receives a great deal of attention on its own in the literature and probably should be accorded separate focus. Thinking back to the job characteristics model of work motivation (Fig. 1.5), we noted at the beginning of this chapter that one way principals can influence the degree to which teachers *experience and feel responsible for work outcomes* is to involve teachers in decisions which affect their daily work. In this section, we will examine why teacher participation in decision-making is important, consider a model of participation in decision-making, and discuss the practical applications of this model to your work as a building principal.

Why participate? Participation is defined in Owens (1991) as a person's emotional and mental involvement in a group situation which stimulates him/her to contribute to and share responsibility for group goals. The notion of ownership in decisions flows directly from mental and emotional involvement and suggests that persons who participate in decisions will accept greater responsibility for the decision and "making it work"; in contrast, those who give consent to a decision without participating in the process are less likely to buy into the decision and its implementation. As Owens further suggests, participation motivates individuals to release their energy, talent, and creativity in making and implementing the decision.

Is participation in decision-making an end in itself? I don't think so. I concur with Owens (1991) that participation in decision-making should lead to better decisions and result in professional growth and development of the participants.

On its face, however, teacher participation in decision-making seems to be desirable. Hoy and Miskel (1991) offer generalizations derived from research and theoretical literature which summarize the effects of teacher participation in decision-making:

- Participation in formulating school policies is generally related to teacher morale and enthusiasm for the school organization.
- Participation in decision-making is positively related to teachers' satisfaction with the teaching profession.
- Principals who involve teachers in decision-making are more favorably viewed by teachers than principals who do not involve teachers.

- Teachers neither desire nor expect to be involved in every decision; accordingly, too much or too little involvement can be equally harmful.
- The roles and functions of teachers and administrators vary according to the nature of the decision problem.
- In order to maximize the effectiveness of participatory decision-making, the principal must consider the following questions:
  - Under what conditions should teachers be involved?
  - To what extent and how should teachers be involved?
  - How should the decision-making group be constituted?
  - What role is most effective for the principal? (p. 328)

Based on these four questions and on the assumption that the decision-making process involves (Bridges, 1967; Hoy & Miskel, 1991) (1) **defining** a problem, (2) **specifying** alternative solutions, (3) **predicting** consequences for each alternative solution, and (4) **selecting** from the best alternative solution, we will examine a decision-making model which, surprisingly, has been around for quite some time, but which still has practical application to your work as a principal.

A SHARED DECISION-MAKING MODEL

This decision-making model was first offered by Edwin M. Bridges (1967) as a model for principals to consider in implementing shared decision-making in their schools. A modified depiction of this model is shown in Figure 2.1 [This model is adapted from Bridges and Hoy & Miskel (1991).] While this model is not prescriptive, implying a "one-best" way to involve teachers in decision-making, it provides a framework for you to consider in thinking about how to foster such participation.

This model assumes that not every decision calls for shared decision-making. However, it also acknowledges the need for participation in decision-making and considers the four questions elaborated on the preceding page. We will consider the facets of this model in answering these four questions.

Under what conditions should teachers be involved? The concept which "drives" this model is *zone of acceptance*, which is the degree to which teachers will accept an administrator's decisions unquestionably; thus, as Figure 2.1 suggests, the greater the degree to which a decision falls within teachers' zone of acceptance, the less likely it is necessary to involve teachers in the decision-making process.

Figure 2.1 also suggests that there are two "tests" which influence the degree to which a decision lies within or outside teachers' zone of acceptance; by application, principals can use these tests to assess their teachers' zone of acceptance These two tests are:

- *Test of Relevance*: The degree to which teachers' personal stakes in the decision are high. For example, science teachers have little at stake in decisions involving the business education program. However, all teachers (regardless of subject matter affiliation) have a personal stake in decisions involving a school's discipline management program.
- *Test of Expertise*: The degree to which teachers are able to contribute to the decision by virtue of experience and knowledge. For example, teachers in the social studies department are less likely to be able to contribute expertise to a decision regarding the computer science curriculum. However, all teachers are more likely to contribute expertise to a decision regarding a new method for teacher evaluation.

When we examine both tests simultaneously, we logically arrive at four "decision situations" as illustrated in Figure 2.1. Each situation and an example are elaborated below.

- *Situation I*. In this situation, the decision is ***clearly within teachers' zone of acceptance*** as illustrated by no relevance and no expertise. For example, decisions regarding administrative extra-curricular duty assignments might fall within the zone. Thus, teachers **do not need to be involved** in this decision. To involve teachers in this situation would only cause the principal to waste teachers' time and could result in their alienation.

- *Situation II.* In this situation, the decision is ***marginally within teachers' zone of acceptance*** as evidenced by little or no expertise but high relevance. For example, the principal might seek teacher involvement in a decision regarding developing a new computerized attendance accounting program. Clearly, teachers have a high personal stake in the result of the accounting program (to the degree it saves teachers valuable instructional time in taking daily attendance), yet probably do not have the technical expertise to design the program. In Situation II, the involvement of the teachers is **occasional**, should probably occur toward the end of the decision-making process, and should depend on the decision problem as well as the issues elaborated in the next three questions. The principal's likely desire to involve teachers in the decision process is to gain teacher acceptance of the final decision to aid implementation.
- *Situation III.* In this situation, the decision is ***clearly outside teachers' zone of acceptance*** as evidenced by high expertise and high relevance. For example, an elementary school principal might wish to revise the entire reading program. Certainly, the elementary school teachers have both expertise and relevance in this situation. As such, involvement should be **frequent** and at all four steps of the decision process.
- *Situation IV.* In this situation, the decision is again ***marginally within teachers' zone of acceptance*** as evidenced by high expertise but little or no relevance. For example, the principal might seek teacher involvement in a decision regarding purchasing curriculum management software for teachers in core academic classes. The principal might wish to involve computer science teachers to test prospective software for troubleshooting capabilities; in this case, the computer science teachers might have relatively high expertise, but probably have little personal stake in the outcome of the decision. The computer science teachers' involvement in this decision should be **occasional**, should probably

FIGURE 2.1. SHARED DECISION MAKING MODEL

Test of Expertise (Capable of Contributing)	Yes — **Test of Relevance** (Personal stake in decision)	No — **Test of Relevance** (Personal stake in decision)
No	*Situation II* **MARGINALLY WITHIN ZONE OF ACCEPTANCE** **INVOLVEMENT:** ***Occasional*** **DECISION-MAKING ARRANGEMENT:** Democratic-centralist	*Situation I* **CLEARLY WITHIN ZONE OF ACCEPTANCE** **INVOLVEMENT:** ***Never*** **DECISION-MAKING ARRANGEMENT:** Not applicable
Yes	*Situation III* **CLEARLY OUTSIDE ZONE OF ACCEPTANCE** **INVOLVEMENT:** ***Frequent*** **DECISION-MAKING ARRANGEMENT:** Parliamentarian or Participant-determining	*Situation IV* **MARGINALLY WITHIN ZONE OF ACCEPTANCE** **INVOLVEMENT:** ***Occasional*** **DECISION-MAKING ARRANGEMENT:** Democratic-centralist

DECISION PROCESS

1. **Define** problem
2. **Specify** alternative soluations
3. **Predict** consequences of alternatives
4. **Select** from best alternative

be early in the decision process, and should depend on the decision problem as well as the issues elaborated in the next three questions. The principal's likely desire to involve teachers in the decision process is to reach a better quality decision.

Since previously-cited research suggests that teachers neither expect nor desire to be involved in every decision, the application is clear. Without considering teachers' zone of acceptance and the tests of relevance and expertise, principals run the risk of alienating and frustrating teachers by either (1) involving teachers in decision which clearly fall within the zone of acceptance or (2) not involving teachers in decisions which clearly fall outside the zone of acceptance.

To what extent and how should teachers be involved? In other words, what is the role of teachers in the decision-making process and at what stages of the four-step decision-making process should teachers become involved? The degree to which teachers should be involved and the roles of teachers are examined in light of this four step process *in conjunction with* (1) the freedom and authority granted to the decision-making team by the principal at each stage of the process (see Note) and (2) the zone of acceptance of teachers. Essentially, the principal defines the role of the teachers at each stage according to the freedom and authority he/she grants to the decision-making team and the teachers' zone of acceptance. The 4-step process with a brief explanation of how the principal defines the roles of teachers is offered below.

- **Defining** the problem. At this stage, the actions of the principal (and thus the decision-making team) can range from defining the problem him/herself based on information collected to the team gathering the information and defining the problem as a team. Certainly, there is no need to involve staff if the principal is defining the problem.
- **Specifying** alternative solutions. At this stage, the actions of the principal can range from developing a list of alternative solutions to calling upon the team to develop alternative solutions.
- **Predicting** the consequences of each alternative solu-

tion. The actions range from the principal unilaterally predicting the consequences to the team predicting the consequences.

- **Selecting** from the best alternative solution. At this stage, the principal can make the decision unilaterally, make the decision after considering recommendations from the team, or delegate the final decision-making authority to the team. Certainly, the principal must be willing to accept a team's decision if he/she is willing to grant final decision-making authority to the team. Bridges (1967, p. 55) makes it clear that "Regardless of the route the principal takes, it is important for him to *make quite clear to the teachers the boundaries of their authority and the area of freedom in which they can operate*" (emphasis in original).

To reiterate, the role of the principal and teachers depends on: (a) each stage of the decision-making process, (b) the zone of acceptance of the teachers involved in the process, and (c) the degree of authority and freedom granted to the team by the principal. By application, in a Situation III scenario, the role and authority of the teachers should be greater than the role and authority of teachers in a Situation II or IV scenario.

As Bridges (1967) notes, this 4-step decision process is just one of many conceptions of decision-making processes. At a minimum, I would suggest that principals add a fifth and sixth step. Step five would entail implementing the best alternative solution, while step six necessarily involves evaluating the solution implemented. In fact, step six would not only include evaluating the solution, but also evaluating the decision-making process in terms of (1) how the process enabled the decision-making team to reach the decision, and (2) how the process influenced gaining acceptance of the decision.

How should the decision-making group be constituted? Essentially, the questions are this: How will the decision-making team "decide to decide" and how much power does each person on the team exert over the final decision? According to Bridges (1967, p. 55), there are three types of "constitutional arrangements" the principal can use in the decision-making process. These are defined as follows:

- *Democratic-centralist*: In this arrangement, the principal presents a problem to the decision-making team and asks for their input. However, the ***principal makes the final decision***. This type of arrangement is considered to be better suited to Situation II, where the principal wishes to gain acceptance of the decision by the teaching staff because of the decision's high relevance to the staff, and Situation IV, where the principal wishes to improve the quality of the decision by making use of the decision-making team's high expertise.
- *Parliamentarian*: In this arrangement, the entire team makes the final decision, but only a ***majority*** is necessary to gain approval of the decision. This arrangement is better suited to a Situation III decision problem which is outside teachers' zone of acceptance. As a principal, you may wish to use this arrangement if a decision problem is structured such that consensus is quite unlikely, but faculty participation is necessary to gain acceptance or to reach a higher quality decision.
- *Participant-determining*: In this arrangement, the entire team must reach ***consensus*** to approve a decision. This arrangement is also better suited to a Situation III decision problem. The principal may wish to use this arrangement when acceptance or a high quality decision is contingent on consensus, but should keep in mind that reaching consensus is often a "time-consuming, high-energy expenditure process" (Bridges, 1967, p. 56).

These constitutional arrangements are not prescriptive, but serve to inform you as a principal when "deciding how the team will decide."

What role is most effective for the principal? The principal's role will vary according to the decision situation and, by application, the constitutional arrangement of the decision-making team. The role of the principal under each arrangement can be summarized as follows:

- *Democratic-centralist*: As noted earlier, this constitutional arrangement is most useful in decision Situations II and

IV, when a decision problem is marginally within teachers' zone of acceptance, and the principal uses shared decision-making to either gain acceptance of the decision (Situation II) or to reach a higher quality decision (Situation IV). Under these arrangements, the role of the principal would be to define and present the decision problem to the decision-making team and seek the team's input before making the decision. In Situation II, where teachers and the decision-making team have little expertise but have a high personal stake in the decision (much like the computerized attendance program situation), the principal is probably well advised to involve the team in stages 3 and 4 of the decision process to gain acceptance of the decision from the entire staff. In this situation, the role of the principal would be to explain the rationale for the decision alternatives and seek the reaction of the team to each alternative; keep in mind, however, that principal retains authority to make the final decision. In Situation IV, where teachers and the decision-making team have little at stake personally but can contribute expertise to the decision problem (much like the computer science teachers who will evaluate the trouble shooting capabilities of curriculum management software in core academic areas), the principal is probably well advised to involve the team earlier in the decision process to help define the problem and specify alternative solutions to the problem. In this situation, the role of the principal would be to facilitate open communication within the team to enhance the quality of the decision to purchase software, and to focus on the process of making the decision rather than to specify a solution (especially since the expertise of the decision team is necessary to reach a higher quality decision).

- *Parliamentarian*: This arrangement is best suited to Situation III decision problems, which are clearly outside teachers' zone of acceptance (recall our example of the elementary principal's desire to revise the entire elementary school reading program). However, the decision team makes the final decision by a majority vote. Under this arrangement, the role of the principal is clearly to make sure that all viewpoints are aired and considered so that all issues are "on the table" prior to the vote, and that after the vote the team can agree to support and implement the decision.

- *Participant-determining*: Recall that this arrangement is also used in Situation III decision problems falling clearly outside teachers' zone of acceptance. Under this arrangement, a *consensus* is necessary to choose the best decision alternative. As implied earlier, this type of arrangement is probably the least realistic and should only be used if it is absolutely necessary to reach consensus to implement the final decision. In this arrangement, the role of the principal is to build consensus by remaining neutral, by facilitating open communication, and by finding similarities in opposing viewpoints on which to reach consensus.

I chose this decision-making model for several reasons. ***First***, it makes sense. It seems that we are on a participation in decision-making bandwagon, almost following the "Involve Everyone in Everything" advice from Peters (1988, p. 285). This model establishes common sense and research-supported criteria for deciding whom to involve. ***Second***, it is usable. I believe that principals can use this model both to reflect on previous shared decision-making situations in their buildings and to inform future shared decision-making initiatives. ***Third***, this model talks about "deciding how to decide." This planning issue is vitally important to consider *prior to* embarking on the decision process and constituting the decision-making group. ***Finally***, the model suggests roles for the principal to assume for each decision situation and constitutional arrangement. For these reasons, I think this model has the application that is necessary to link the "theoretical" with the "practical."

However, this model cannot and should not be considered overly prescriptive. As Hoy and Miskel (1991) suggest:

> This model for shared decision-making is not a panacea. It is not a substitute for sensitive and reflective administrative thought and action; it simply provides

some rough guidelines for determining when and how teachers and principals should be involved in joint decision-making. The effectiveness of decisions is determined by both the quality of the decision and the acceptance and commitment of subordinates to implement the decision. (p. 332)

For your use, I have included two practical guides. The first is a sample memorandum and checklist which might aid you in determining teachers' zones of acceptance for decision issues that may surface in your building (See Fig. 2.2). This checklist is not a research proven, psychometrically "pure" instrument, but I hope that you can use it to assess your teachers' zones of acceptance. As other issues surface which call for shared decision-making, please feel free to modify this checklist to tailor it to your work.

FIGURE 2.2. SHARED DECISION-MAKING PREFERENCE CHECKLIST & COVER MEMORANDUM

October 26, 1995
MEMORANDUM
TO: Anywhere School Staff
FROM: I.M. Principal
RE: Decision Teams

As part of our effort to facilitate shared decision-making in our building, I am sending you a copy of the Decision-Making Preference Checklist. Please let me know your degree of interest in participating in decision teams which will address the issues listed below. Please indicate your interest participation by circling "Yes" or "No" under each issue. If you circle yes, please respond to whether you can contribute "Expertise," "Personal Relevance" (i.e., whether the decision is personally relevant), or both to the decision team. Please be confident that only I will review your responses, and that your responses will be used only to provide me direction in composing decision-making teams as these issues become pertinent. Thanks for your time and energy!

Decision-making Preference Checklist

Decision Issue	Interest		Contribution	
Curriculum Design/ Revision	Yes	No	Expertise	Personal Relevance

Textbook Selection	Yes	No	Expertise	Personal Relevance
Student Discipline Policies & Procedures	Yes	No	Expertise	Personal Relevance
Student Attendance Policies & Procedures	Yes	No	Expertise	Personal Relevance
Faculty Inservice Planning/ Staff Development	Yes	No	Expertise	Personal Relevance
Campus/District Goal-setting and Planning	Yes	No	Expertise	Personal Relevance
Instructional Issues	Yes	No	Expertise	Personal Relevance
New Teacher Induction	Yes	No	Expertise	Personal Relevance
Student Academic Placement Policies & Procedures	Yes	No	Expertise	Personal Relevance
Grievances Procedures	Yes	No	Expertise	Personal Relevance
Master Scheduling	Yes	No	Expertise	Personal Relevance
Faculty Duty Assignments	Yes	No	Expertise	Personal Relevance
Budgeting/School Expenditures	Yes	No	Expertise	Personal Relevance

The second practical guide is courtesy of Julie Combs, principal of Woodrow Wilson Elementary School in the Coppell (Texas) Independent School District (see Fig. 2.3). Dr. Combs uses this checklist to plan for decision-making at Wilson. This checklist is organized around decision-making issues that she encounters on periodic bases (I have included several issues for illustrative purposes). The columns to the left of the decision issues indicate who might have or share in responsibility for decision-making. And of course, the check marks indicate who actually has or shares in the responsibility for decision-making. The rest of the checklist is self-explanatory, and should be modified to fit your specific needs.

FIGURE 2.3. DECISION-MAKING PLANNING CHECKLIST
(Courtesy of and adapted from Julie Combs, principal of Woodrow Wilson Elementary School, Coppell Independent School District, Coppell, Texas)

Responsibility				Decision-Making Issue
O	P	T	SB	
	✓		✓	Selecting School Goals
	✓	✓	✓	Recruiting applicants for school (Job Fair)
	✓		✓	Develop master schedule
	✓	✓	✓	Use of alternative assessments in grades/school
✓	✓	✓		K-5 handwriting program

Key:
- O Other decision-making body (e.g., school board, central office, etc.)
- P Principal
- T Grade level or other campus-based teams
- SB Site-based decision-making team

SUMMARY

In this chapter we examined the principal's role in creating conditions which foster teamwork, collegiality, and participation. We noted that principals create conditions for teachers to *experience that their work is meaningful* in part by creating teams and fostering collegiality. Collegiality is characterized by commitment to shared purposes and mutual respect for the talents and motives of teammates. In addition, principals create conditions for teachers to *experience and feel responsibility for work outcomes* in part by involving teachers in decisions which affect their daily work.

To foster teamwork and collegiality, we examined a series of strategies that principals can use to create the conditions that result in a "working, breathing" team environment. To involve teachers in decision-making, we examined a model which addressed four questions that principals should consider in fostering effective shared decision-making. Finally, we provided a checklist for principals to use to assess teachers' zone of acceptance in school-based decision issues.

ACTION PLAN

- Examine your vision for your school. Do your teachers buy into the vision? If not, is the concern with you, the staff, the vision, or combinations thereof?
- Examine your own expectations for teamwork and collegiality. Are you modeling these expectations?
- Assess your staff's readiness for teamwork.
- Examine your school's organizational and physical structure. Are there obvious barriers to teamwork which can readily be removed?
- Assess recent shared decision-making efforts which were successful and unsuccessful in light of the Shared Decision-Making Model (Fig. 2.1). What facets of the model contributed to the success or failure of the efforts?
- Assess individual staff member's zones of acceptance using the checklist provided (modify as necessary). Use this information to enhance future shared decision-making efforts.

SUGGESTED READINGS

Bridges, E.M. (1967). A model for shared decision-making in the school principalship. *Educational Administration Quarterly, 3,* 49-61. (A classic, but readable and well worth reading).

Sergiovanni, T.J. (1992). *Moral leadership: Getting to the heart of school improvement.* San Francisco, CA: Jossey-Bass. (See especially Chapter 7 titled "Collegiality as a Professional Virtue").

NOTE

Covey (1989) provides an excellent framework for principals to consider in thinking about delegation of freedom and authority; this framework can also be applied to granting authority and freedom in the decision-making process. Called "Stewardship Delegation" (p. 173), this type of delegation focuses on results rather than methods, and is in direct contrast to "Gofer Delegation" (p. 173), which focuses on methods rather than results. According to Covey, stewardship delegation involves clarifying mutual understandings and expectations around five areas (I have included some applications to the principal in the decision-making process):

- *Desired results.* In the decision-making process, the principal and the decision-making team should clarify up-front exactly what should be accomplished as a result of the decision. For example, in a decision to recommend admissions criteria for an elementary school gifted and talented program, is the desired result to legitimately identify gifted students or to pacify community power bases within the school?
- *Parameters.* The principal and the decision-making team should identify parameters within which the team should function. As we noted in the text of the discussion, who retains final authority for making the decision? What are the legal, ethical, and cultural (i.e., norms of the school) parameters within which the team must operate? What are the pitfalls to avoid at each step of the decision-making model? What are the mistakes which have been made in the past and how can the team learn from them?
- *Resources.* In this case, the principal and the team should identify the time, financial, technical, human, and organizational resources which can be used in the decision-making process. For example, in a high school which is considering converting to a form of block scheduling, does the decision-making team have the time and financial resources to gather information by visiting other schools which have adopted block scheduling?
- *Accountability.* In this area, the principal and the decision-making team establish the standards against which the decision will be evaluated. If the decision

involves revising job qualifications for hiring new teachers in a particular building, the standard against which the decision will be evaluated might include a measure of the first year performance of first-year teachers hired under the revised qualifications.

- *Consequences.* Here, the principal and the decision-making team detail both intended and unintended consequences resulting from the evaluation. In the example on revising admissions criteria for the elementary school gifted and talented program, an intended consequence most likely was to identify students who were truly gifted. Unintended consequences could be positive, e.g., gifted and talented students performing even better than expected on measures of performance. Conversely, unintended consequences could be negative, e.g., dealing with the "political fallout" from parents who thought their students should have been admitted to the program.

Once again, these five areas under stewardship delegation provide the principal with another way of thinking about how, and how much freedom and authority he or she is willing to grant to a decision-making team.

3

Providing Challenging Work Roles, Intellectual Stimulation, and Autonomy

"Teachers have occupied a subordinate position in matters of technical knowledge. They are prepared for their work . . . and once they are employed, major instructional decisions are made by school boards and administrators."
Lortie, 1975, p. 240

"You mean to tell me that I have 18 hours of college calculus and I'm teaching consumer math?"
Unidentified teacher, circa 1985

"I've been teaching to this damned test all month."
Unidentified teacher, circa 1995

In spite of what we claim to know about motivation and motivating others, we still have a long way to go to create conditions of work that provide challenging work roles, intellectual stimulation, and autonomy. Sergiovanni (1992, p. 64) probably captures the point best:

> Sometimes flow just happens as teachers close the classroom door and, on their own, get into the rhythm of their work. But the obstacles are too great for this to happen often enough. In many schools, for example, teaching is heavily scripted by a bureaucratic system that programs what teachers do, when they do it, how they do it, and even why. Few teachers following a script are challenged to work anywhere near their abilities. By the same token, we often give some teachers, particularly new ones, responsibilities for which they are not ready. Teaching jobs are often fragmented and compartmentalized. This makes it difficult for teachers to sense the wholeness of what they are doing. Schedules are beyond their reach. Curricula are mandated from afar. Materials and books are selected by someone else. Teaching is routinized to the point where it becomes habit. And to make it all work, "what gets rewarded gets done" is a rule that is firmly entrenched as the only motivational strategy.

As bleak as this landscape looks, I do not believe that it is hopeless. In spite of the conditions described above (which, sadly, do not seem likely to disappear anytime soon), there are school districts and schools where teachers are intellectually stimulated, are presented with or are creating challenging work roles, and are afforded or are creating autonomy. The common denominator in such schools is leadership which creates these job conditions so that teachers experience that their work is meaningful and experience responsibility for the outcomes of their work.

As we continue to note, principals can create conditions by which teachers experience and feel that their work is meaningful by designing jobs which enable teachers to utilize a variety of talent and skills (*skill variety*) and perform complete rather than isolated tasks (*task identity*). To enhance skill variety and task identity, teacher work activities must be intellectually stimulating and challenging. At the same time, principals can enhance the degree to which teachers experience and feel responsible for the outcomes of their work by providing teachers with appropriate autonomy to schedule and carry out work activities. How principals can create these job conditions is the subject of this chapter.

THE FLOW OF WORK

While reading various books and articles to help prepare this book, I came across a different perspective of intrinsic motivation that, when applied to work, resembles the job characteristics model. However, this perspective seems to better "get at" the intellectual stimulation and challenging work roles necessary to enhance experienced work meaningfulness as well as the autonomy necessary to enhance responsibility for work outcomes. This perspective is the work of Mihaly Csikszentmihalyi and is elaborated in his 1990 work titled *Flow*. Briefly, Csikszentmihalyi initially interviewed hundreds of experts such as surgeons, musicians, artists, athletes, etc., that is, people who spent time participating in activities of their preference and derived optimal enjoyment from these activities. From the accounts of experts who were doing exactly what they wanted to be doing, Csikszentmihalyi determined that these experts experienced a particular state of mind when participating in these activities. He described this optimal state as flow and defined it as ". . . the state in which people are so involved in an activity that nothing else seems to matter; the experience itself is so enjoyable that people will do it even at great cost, for the sheer sake of doing it" (1990, p. 4).

Now, what might appear obvious is that these experts probably experienced this state of flow largely because they were highly gifted, well trained, and probably well compensated for their activities. However, in subsequent research around the world, Csikszentmihalyi found that this state of flow existed in people from all walks of life who reported optimal experiences, regardless of their social class, cultural status, age, gender, etc.

Briefly, what are the components of this state of flow which exist when individuals optimally enjoy one of life's activities? Csikszentmihalyi (1990) identified the following eight components:

- An activity which is challenging, yet which people have a chance of completing.
- An activity in which a person's concentration is completely absorbed.
- An activity with clear goals.
- An activity which provides immediate feedback.
- An activity characterized by "deep and effortless involvement" (p. 49) requiring the individual to set aside other worries of everyday life.
- An activity which allows individuals to exercise control over their own actions.
- An activity in which concern for one's self disappears but a greater sense of self results.
- An activity which alters one's sense of the duration of time; hours seem like minutes, and minutes seem like hours.

At first glance it seems evident that several of these flow components are closely related to intellectual stimulation, challenging work roles, and autonomy. Activities which are challenging yet attainable, which call for complete concentration, and which are characterized by a deep involvement are more likely to provide intellectual stimulation and challenge than activities without these components. Similarly, activities which allow individuals to exercise control over their actions provide autonomy.

When it comes to school and the flow of work, there are two possibilities that exist in order for teachers to experience this flow. First, teachers may arrive at the work situation with an "autotelic personality" (Csikszentmihalyi, 1990, p. 149), defined as "the ability to create flow experiences even in the most barren environment. . . ." Now, we know that there are some people who arrive at work daily with this type of personality; in fact, many of them are teachers, perhaps on your staff. However, we are kidding ourselves if we think that all educators (principals included!) are autotelic in nature. Yet we could try to transform teachers' personalities into autotelic personalities. A second possible way for teachers to experience flow is to change the conditions of the job so that the job itself becomes autotelic. By arranging jobs which provide challenge, intellectual stimulation, and autonomy, it is possible for the principal to increase the likelihood that teachers will experience work flow. While it is probably easier to change job conditions than it is to transform personalities, Csikszentmihalyi suggests that these two strategies are complementary. Accordingly, the principal should focus both on: (1) designing jobs which contain these flow components and (2) developing teachers so that they set clear goals, recognize and seize opportunities to undertake challenging activities with attainable goals, and develop skills necessary to achieve the goals and experience work flow.

PROVIDING CHALLENGING WORK ROLES

Isn't teaching in itself challenging enough? Without a doubt. Yet, there are at least two types of challenges that teachers in our schools face daily. First, and often the most obvious, is the challenge of "making it through the day." This challenge is probably more predominant in schools characterized by student social and behavioral problems and by lack of support (e.g., financial, parental, moral, administrative or board). The second type of challenge is more likely to occur in schools where teachers are less concerned about making it through the day, yet do not find much challenge in their jobs. This lack of challenge is more attributable to the structure of the job itself and is what I would like to address.

What are the strategies that principals can use to create challenging work roles among the staff and enhance teachers' flow experiences? There is no magic "list" of strategies, but based on a lot of reading and talking with principals, I have compiled the following strategies for consideration:

- **Assess the teachers' perceptions** of the extent to which teaching roles are structured to be challenging. Look particularly at veteran teachers who have been in the same teaching assignment for years to see if they perceive that their jobs are not challenging.
- **Recruit, select, and develop** teachers who welcome challenge. Our teacher preparation programs are producing better qualified teachers every year. Each of us

has been a first-year teacher; I have yet to run across a first year teacher who, although somewhat apprehensive, was not enthusiastic and did not believe that he or she could change the world. As principals, we need to use this enthusiasm and idealism better than we have in the past. Our inservice programs for teachers need to develop and add new skills so that teachers possess the skill variety to meet work challenges.

- **Continually assess teacher skill levels and balance these skills levels against the level of challenge the job provides.** Notice that I did not suggest matching the skill level with the level of challenge. Teachers must certainly have the skills to meet the challenge; more importantly, teachers must *believe* they have the skills to meet the challenge. At the same time, the activity must be challenging enough so that teachers' entire skill repertoire will be used to meet the task. It is as if the activity is challenging to the point that it is just beyond the individual's reach, yet the person has the skills to carry out the activity. Perhaps this balance can best be illustrated by watching a two and one-half year old child meet challenge after challenge with skills she does not quite realize she possesses. At the playground you can see her meet challenges such as climbing up a set of monkey bars, hanging down by her arms from a bar parallel to the ground, and dropping to the ground and landing on her feet. The child had been able to climb the bars for some time before she realized that she had the strength and coordination to hang down and drop to the ground. The same can be said for the skill-challenge balance in many activities.

  Obviously, the principal must be able to attain this balance for teachers in the building, first by recognizing teachers' skill levels. If a teacher's skill level is not up to the challenge, placing a teacher in an overly challenging situation will harm both students and the teacher, produce anxiety in the teacher, and cause the teacher to seek less challenging activities rather than focus on skill improvement. Conversely, if a teacher's skill level exceeds the level of the challenge, the teacher can not only become bored, but can also lose skills previously developed (see, for example, the math teacher cited at the beginning of the chapter).

- **Design and enrich teacher work roles** so that these roles require a variety of challenges rather than repetitive activities. Please do not confuse job enrichment with job enlargement (Kaiser, 1982); although enrichment may entail additional activities, it does not suggest additional repetitive activities. For example, I know of too many schools where first year teachers are rewarded for their enthusiasm and idealism by teaching a grade level or class preparation that nobody else wants. Concurrently, veteran teachers are often entrenched in assignments (such as gifted and talented grade level classes or advanced placement classes) reserved only for those who have "done their time." Both arrangements are counterproductive. Principals should strive for a balance. Assign, or even better yet, *ask* beginning teachers with what type of students they work best, and what they would like to teach; within the school's mission, honor their requests. In addition, ask and even *insist* that veteran teachers try something different. In my view, no teacher should teach the same grade level or preparation year after year; at the same time, no teacher should be burdened with too many simultaneous preparations.

  One strategy to design work roles to make them more challenging *and* to reduce isolation among teachers is to find ways for teachers to work together within and across disciplines. Within grade levels or disciplines, team planning and teaching seems to be one effective strategy to reduce isolation and to see how other and perhaps more effective teachers are meeting challenges. Multi-disciplinary teaming, long a trademark among elementary school teachers and more recently so among middle school teachers, has the effect of providing teachers with the perspective of how the "whole" student is progressing and how curricular areas relate to each other. Particularly in large high schools, I see this as a largely undeveloped strategy which can reduce both teacher and student isolation.

Isolation is particularly acute for beginning teachers. I believe it is imperative to find ways for beginning teachers to see beyond the perspective of the classroom door. Beginning teachers should have constant opportunities to be paired with qualified mentor teachers, to observe effective teachers within and outside the building, to attend meaningful professional development meetings, and to become involved in district level activities such as curriculum writing, long-range planning, and other important committee work.

Principals must be keenly aware of the skill/challenge balance in new teachers and be willing to go above and beyond to assist these teachers. My first year as a mathematics teacher was particularly difficult, since I reported to work five weeks after the beginning of the school year due to military commitments. Consequently, I inherited four classes (three different preparations) of students who were accustomed to another teacher. Under any circumstances, the first year of teaching is difficult; under these circumstances, it was nearly enough to convince me to try something different. Were it not for Harold Devine, an assistant principal and my instructional supervisor who recognized the skill/challenge imbalance and helped me tremendously, I might very likely have tried something different. Again, quality leadership matters.

- **Constantly provide teachers with opportunities and support to develop their skill levels and utilize the skills of teachers to facilitate professional development**. The old "sit and git" model of professional development, still alive and well in many places, must be replaced as the predominant model. As educators, we are constantly implored to tailor instruction (to the extent possible) to the individual needs of students, yet we so often fail to follow this advice in professional development. Professional development takes an infinite number of forms including, but not limited to, reading, attending professional development conferences, writing, conducting a seminar for colleagues, planning professional development activities, and peer observation. If principals are to be aware of the skill/challenge balance for teachers, realizing that this balance will be different for each teacher, then principals must seek ways to involve teachers in planning professional development activities and to tailor development activities that are meaningful to teachers.

In many ways (and speaking as a teacher), teachers are the toughest audience for which an "expert" (once defined by John Hoyle of Texas A&M University as someone who comes in from a distance greater than 50 miles) can conduct a staff development session. I think I have finally figured it out: In many cases, teachers are tough because (1) they are not hearing anything useful or new and would rather be spending their time on more constructive activities, and (2) they might better be able to conduct the development than the expert, who probably has little appreciation for the context of the school or the district. I believe that there is an untapped reservoir of talent right in front of our eyes when it comes to professional development activities in our own buildings. What better way for a teacher to experience skill variety, task identity, and task significance than to conduct a seminar for his or her colleagues.

Finally, principals can play a substantial role in facilitating staff development activities by providing support (not just limited to financial support, but also released time, recognition, etc.) for teachers engaged in professional development activities.

PROVIDING INTELLECTUAL STIMULATION

Coupled with a work role that is challenging is one which should be intellectually stimulating. Again, I emphasize *should*. For example, while it might be challenging to teach five classes of the same subject daily or the grade level that no one else wants, I would argue that there are other more intellectually stimulating ways to structure a teacher's daily routine.

During graduate school, I often had the opportunity to listen to Dean Corrigan, former dean of the college of education at Texas A&M University, talk about schools and teachers. I particularly remember that "Dean Dean" would become flushed with passion when he talked about how public schools should be centers of inquiry for both students *and* teachers. Teachers in inquiry schools engage in meaningful dialogue on how to improve curriculum and instruction, conduct action research to inform and solve problems of practice, share their findings with colleagues within and outside of the school, participate in planning and decision-making on issues that are relevant to their practice, plan and conduct professional development activities, collaborate with university and other professional colleagues to improve practice, mentor their teacher colleagues, and on and on. Put succinctly, teachers in inquiry schools are engaged in activities not only within, but beyond, the classroom which provide both a challenge and intellectual stimulation.

What role does the principal play in providing teachers with intellectually stimulating work? I believe that the principal's role involves three facets: (1) Recognizing and seeking opportunities for teachers to engage in intellectually stimulating work activities, (2) providing support for teachers to engage in these activities (see Chapter 4 for more on providing support), and (3) recognizing teachers for participating in these activities (see Chapter 6). There are probably more opportunities, both in and beyond the building, for intellectual stimulation than we realize. Consider, for example, the following activities:

- **Encouraging and providing support for teachers to write about a successful curricular innovation or teaching practice**, perhaps even **presenting this innovation** or practice to the entire staff or at a professional meeting, or **even publishing the practice or innovation** (there is very little professionally that compares to seeing one's name in print!).
- **Encouraging and providing support for teachers to engage in textbook review and selection, curriculum writing, instructional improvement, peer coaching, designing teacher and administrative evaluation sys-**

tems, student policy involvement, and student activities.

- **Recommending teachers for district level committees** such as long-range planning, community involvement, etc. One caveat: Avoid recommending the same teachers. Our early-career teachers need opportunities to expand their horizons!
- **Encouraging and providing support for teachers to attend professional meetings** and then **asking them to present what they have learned** to their team, department, or to the entire faculty. Of course, recognition for these activities is vital!
- **Encouraging and providing support for teachers to engage in action research projects**. Action research is research conducted by practitioner-scholars to both understand and improve problems of professional practice. The term practitioner-scholar is one frequently used by Jim McNamara, professor at Texas A&M University and former executive director of the Texas A&M School/University Research Collaborative. The term practitioner-scholar, in my view, really captures the essence of educators in schools of inquiry.

  One of several projects of the Texas A&M School/University Research Collaborative (now housed at the University of Houston) was the teacher-as-researcher project. In this project, public school teachers and university professors collaborated on action research projects of mutual interest to both the teacher and the professor. With financial and in-kind (i.e., released time, meeting space, etc.) support provided both by school districts and the university, teachers and professors would meet frequently throughout the term of the action research projects to plan, conduct, and write up the findings of the research project. Moreover, research findings were presented at an annual conference sponsored by member school districts and the university.

  Having been involved as a research associate with the Collaborative, I was able to see the effects that this project had on teachers and professors. Borg, Gall, and

Gall (1993) nicely summarize these effects as the following:

- Knowing that research findings contribute to the knowledge base for improving professional practice
- Enhancing teachers' professional development and feelings of efficacy
- Providing a collegial network of fellow teacher researchers
- Enhancing teachers' research skills, particularly in the area of defining problems of research interest
- Demystifying the process and the skills of research.

Of course, the notion of teacher action research projects sounds great; yet, there are four conditions which must exist or be created in order for teachers to be able to successfully conduct action research (Borg et al., 1993). These conditions are *time*, *autonomy*, *opportunity*, and *commitment*. If this type of intellectually stimulating work (and it is intellectually stimulating) is important to principals, then principals can greatly influence these four conditions.

By the way, teachers are not the only ones who can carry out action research!

PROVIDING AUTONOMY

Consider the following scenarios. Is each teacher describing a condition of autonomy?

Scenario one. I am a department chair in the middle of my tenth year of public school teaching. Within the organizational framework of my school, I have a considerable amount of discretion over my work and the work of teachers in my department. My principal works with me to arrange teaching schedules so that, to the extent possible, teacher subject expertise and preferences are accommodated. Within curricular guidelines, teachers in my department exercise a great deal of professional latitude regarding teaching methods, instructional materials, and evaluation procedures. Although we have a building and district-wide student behavior management system in place, teachers in my department are responsible for student behavior and are supported by the principal when it comes to handling behavior matters and when it comes to referring student behavioral problems to the principal.

Scenario two. I am a first year public school teacher and have just completed the first six weeks of teaching in my building. I think I'm off to a pretty good start, but some times it's hard to tell. I have my own classroom, and it's really well furnished and is a place where I would like to be a student. We don't have a grade level office, so I don't get to spend a lot of time talking to my grade level colleagues. When I close the classroom door, I'm free to teach as I prefer. Although my undergraduate degree is in early childhood education, I was placed in a sixth grade classroom, even though I told the principal in my interview that I felt more comfortable starting out with younger students. My principal told me that he believes that teachers should have autonomy in the classroom and did not believe in "snoopervision." I'll have to take her at her word, since I have not spoken with her—outside of saying "hello"—since the new teacher inservice. One thing's for certain, I can do whatever I want; I just hope my first evaluation is good enough to be offered another probationary contract.

It probably was not terribly difficult to determine which teacher was operating under conditions of autonomy and which teacher was not.

As we have noted earlier, autonomy is "The degree to which the job provides substantial freedom, independence, and discretion to the individual in scheduling the work and in determining the procedures to be used in carrying it out" (Hackman and Oldham, 1976, p. 258). Moreover, it is the core job characteristic which is posited to influence to the degree to which people experience or feel that they have responsibility over the outcomes of their work. As I have implied earlier, autonomy is necessary for a job to provide challenge and intellectual stimulation.

Going back to our two scenarios above, it is evident that the first teacher (the department chair) operated under conditions of autonomy, while the second teacher (the first year teacher), though left alone to teach as he or she wished, was not autonomous as much as he or she was isolated. The first teacher had considerable latitude to schedule carry out individual and departmental work activities and to interact with colleagues while doing so, while the second teacher, though able to do anything he or she wanted, had no control over work activities and was isolated behind the classroom door. Thus, autonomy is not isolation, and teacher isolation should be avoided!

In their study of shared governance schools in Georgia, Blase and Blase (1994, drawing on the work of Rosenholtz, 1989) identified the following two, distinct facets of teacher autonomy:

- Autonomy as "**Freedom from**" intrusion (p. 72), i.e., the ability to carry out work activities without unnecessary interruptions, interventions, inspections, paperwork, disruptive students, etc.
- Autonomy as "**Freedom to**" (p. 72), or the ability, once the freedom from intrusions are removed, to use one's own professional discretion to schedule and carry out work activities.

Freedom from and freedom to can be thought of in the same light as the hygiene and motivators identified by Herzberg and discussed in Chapter 1. Just as the hygiene factors of sufficient salary, benefits, interpersonal relations, type of supervision, administrative policies and attitudes, job security, and working conditions must be in place so that individuals do not experience dissatisfaction, so must autonomy as *freedom from* be in place so that teachers do not feel stuck in their work. Likewise, just as the motivating factors of the work itself, recognition, achievement, advancement, responsibility, and personal and professional growth must be in place to experience satisfaction, so must autonomy as *freedom to* be in place for teachers to enjoy true autonomy.

With these autonomy distinctions in mind, principals are probably more readily able to influence autonomy as *freedom from* than autonomy as *freedom to* by considering the following strategies:

- **Zealously protecting** teacher's planning and instructional time from interruptions and unnecessary duty assignments (see illustration of Ken McKinney in Chapter 2)
- **Reducing the amount of unnecessary paperwork** teachers have to complete and/or read
- **Supporting teachers** in student discipline matters
- **Calling faculty meetings only when necessary** and **restructuring them as staff development activities**
- **Using channels other than faculty meetings to disseminate routine information** (e.g., teacher daily or weekly bulletins, memoranda, public address announcements)

The role of the principal in creating conditions of autonomy as *freedom to* is markedly more difficult, particularly in light of the influence that state mandates, district policies, collective bargaining agreements, or combinations thereof, have on teachers' work. However, the principal's role in providing greater freedom to, is one which must originate from within the principal him or herself. At the core of this role is the way in which the principal views others (Recall our discussion of Theory X and Theory Y in Chapter 1). A principal who views teachers as lazy, unmotivated paycheck collectors will be less likely to expect or grant autonomy than a principal who views teachers as motivated professionals satisfied with the choice of their profession. In addition to a having a positive view of teachers, the principal should:

- **Recognize the training and expertise** of teachers to function as professionals
- **Make sure that the *freedom from* is taken care of so that the *freedom to* can be accomplished**
- **Hold and convey expectations** of teacher autonomy in the recruitment, selection, and development of teachers
- **Assess the readiness** of individual staff to be autonomous and convey expectations accordingly

- **Keep current** on curricular, instructional, legal, and other trends; teachers are more likely to consider principal's suggestions for intervention when they believe that the principal is credible
- **Model expectations for autonomy by involving teachers** in decisions which will affect their work
- As stated earlier in the chapter, **design teacher work roles to be challenging and intellectually stimulating.**

SUMMARY

In this chapter we examined the principal's role in creating job conditions which result in teachers' work roles that are challenging, intellectually stimulating, and autonomous. We noted that principals can create conditions for teachers to experience that their work is meaningful by enabling teachers to utilize a wide variety of talents and skills (*skill variety*) and to perform complete rather than isolated tasks (*task identity*). Moreover, we noted that principals can also create conditions for teachers to experience responsibility for the outcomes of their work by providing teachers with appropriate *autonomy* to schedule and carry out work activities.

After a brief discussion of the flow of work, we discussed strategies that principals can use to create and engender job conditions which foster challenge, intellectual stimulation, and autonomy in teacher work roles. In providing challenging work roles, we paid particular attention to the balance between teachers' skill level and the level of challenge that the job provides. Specifically, we noted that the level of challenge in a job must require a teacher to use his or her full complement of skills. When the level of challenge exceeds the level of skills, the teacher becomes frustrated and seeks less challenging work conditions rather than focusing on skill improvement. When a teacher's skill level exceeds the level of challenge provided by the job, the teacher is likely to become bored and lose skills previously developed.

In providing job conditions with intellectual stimulation, we noted three general roles that the principal can play: (1) Recognizing and seeking opportunities for teachers to engage in intellectually stimulating work activities, (2) providing support for teachers to engage in these activities, and (3) recognizing teachers for participating in these activities. Subsequently, we noted many activities in which teachers can participate to increase intellectual stimulation on the job, paying particular attention to teachers as researchers.

Finally, we noted the role that the principal assumes in creating autonomous work roles among teachers. We first noted the difference between autonomy and isolation, discussed autonomy as *freedom from* and *freedom to* (Blase & Blase, 1994; Rosenholtz, 1989), and specified strategies that principals can use to remove the *freedom from* roadblocks and clear the way for autonomy as *freedom to*.

It by now must seem evident that job conditions of challenge, intellectual stimulation, and autonomy are interdependent and that one truly cannot exist without the other two. In fact, when these job conditions exist (with a couple of others such as feedback and task significance), the teacher can experience the eight components of flow just as any other "expert" referenced by Csikszentmihalyi (1990). In his chapter titled "Work as Flow," Csikszentmihalyi makes repeated reference to surgeons experiencing work flow. He continually refers to surgery as an "autotelic job" (p. 152) because of many of the conditions that are inherently found in the activity: skill variety; challenges which are flexible, appropriate, and call for the application of specialized skills; autonomy; well defined goals; and immediate feedback. Because of the autotelic nature of the activity, an overwhelming number of surgeons consider their work to be the most enjoyable activity in their life.

Yet, as Csikszentmihalyi (1990) points out, not all surgeons are enthusiastic about their jobs. Perhaps some surgeons become bored because the surgery they perform is dull and repetitive, and new challenges are not readily found. Perhaps other surgeons ("supersurgeons," p. 155) just can't seem to find a surgery that is challenging enough or have done the impossible and are unable to find the impossible task again. Perhaps some are frustrated because they have not updated their skills.

The whole point of Csikszentmihalyi's chapter on work flow is that a healthy combination is needed for a leader to create conditions whereby workers can experience flow: that combination is one of creating autotelic job conditions and finding and developing autotelic personalities who can set clear goals, recognize and seize opportunities for work flow, and develop skills necessary to experience work flow. While principals have certain constraints which are probably not part of the surgeon's life, the implications for the principal are clear. Creating work flow entails addressing both job conditions and people conditions, both of which are as challenging as any part of the principal's job.

ACTION PLAN

- Assess individual staff members' perceptions of the challenge, intellectual stimulation, and autonomy provided by the job (See the questionnaire in Chapter 1; see also "The Work Itself as a Substitute for Leadership Inventory" found in Sergiovanni, 1992, pp. 65–66).
- Assess individual staff members' skill level and readiness for autonomy. As we have noted earlier, this level and readiness will not be the same for each teacher.
- For individual staff members, assess the skill level/challenge balance and act appropriately by modifying the challenge and/or providing opportunities for skill development.
- Find at least three ways to immediately increase the intellectual stimulation of teachers' jobs. Involve, to the extent possible, colleagues from outside your building (including teachers from other buildings and university colleagues).
- Reduce the isolation of teachers in your building. Think of three ways to immediately do this.
- Immediately remove "freedom from" autonomy roadblocks so that you can concentrate on autonomy as "freedom to."
- Continue to examine your personal view of staff members. How is this view influencing your willingness to create conditions of flow at work?

SUGGESTED READINGS

Csikszentmihalyi, M. (1990). *Flow: The psychology of optimal experience.* New York: Harper & Row. (See especially Chapter 4 titled "The Conditions of Flow" and Chapter 7 titled "Work as Flow.")

Blase, J., & Kirby, P.C. (1992). *Bringing out the best in teachers: What effective principals do.* Newbury Park, CA: Corwin Press. (See especially Chapter 5 titled "Granting Professional Autonomy.")

Rosenholtz, S.J. (1989). *Teachers' workplace: The social organization of schools.* White Plains, NY: Longman. (See especially Chapter 6 titled "Teacher Commitment.")

Sergiovanni, T.J. (1992). *Moral leadership.* Boston: Allyn & Bacon. (See especially Chapter 5 titled "A State of Flow at Work.")

4

Providing Resources and Supporting Innovation

". . . we are the ones who treat our workers as rote executors. And our first-line supervisors too. We even treat our middle managers as administrators—not creators of a . . . (. . . constantly improving) order." Tom Peters (1988, p. 276) in *Thriving on Chaos*

Although Tom Peters' comment above was aimed primarily at American business, it is not wholly inapplicable to education. In many schools today, teachers and administrators are viewed as rote executors who are bound by or bind themselves by mandated curricular and testing requirements which control instructional strategies and limit instructional innovations. While operating in this environment, principals are expected to be leaders of instruction and agents of change (which I prefer to call school improvement). On the one hand, principals are expected to be innovators and facilitators of innovation; on the other hand, many principals find themselves constrained by or constrain themselves by mandated requirements. On the one hand, principals are to keep abreast of the latest research and school improvement innovations; on the other hand, many principals are victimized by the tendency of our profession to recycle trends and "reinvent the wheel." Finally, we find ourselves in an era of dwindling resources (money, time, space, parental support, public support) which make school improvements all the more challenging.

It is against this backdrop (which thankfully does not exist in all schools) that we examine the role of the principal in providing resources for school improvement and supporting innovation. We will first examine how the principal's role in each area creates conditions for teacher motivation and then discuss strategies that principals can use to effectively function as resource providers and innovation supporters.

PROVIDING RESOURCES

PERSPECTIVES

Although it is intuitively obvious that resources are necessary to sustain the operation of the school, I'm not sure that we often really think about the powerful messages we send through the provision and allocation of resources. To put things in a highly relevant perspective, I am going to assume that all of you either are parents or have parents or have had parents (There, I think I've got everybody!). When we were kids, our parents were the providers of the resources (money, candy, car keys, clothes, toys, entertainment media, etc.). As parents, we are the resource providers. As a teenager, my parents absolutely forbade me (and thankfully so) from attending parties where they thought alcohol was going to be served; thus, they would not provide nor allocate resources (car keys, money, time, etc.) to attend these activities. As parents, we are extremely particular about what our daughter watches on television and provide and allocate television time *and* content judiciously (in fact, during many commercials we switch to the Weather Channel because, quite frankly, we do not want her exposed to the garbage advertised and promoted on most commercials!). Likewise, as children you were subject to parental decisions regarding resource allocation and provision.

Why am I bringing this up? The reason is obvious. As children, we were provided and allocated resources on the basis of priorities that our parents set for us. As parents, we provide and allocate resources for our children based on the priorities we set for them. Simply put, our resources follow what we consider to be important.

Clearly, principals are not parents to teachers, and teachers are not children to be parented. But this analogy certainly holds for the role of the principal in allocating and providing resources. ***The resources that you provide and allocate to teachers signal to teachers what you think is important*** (Yukl, 1989). Please read this again before proceeding.

In addition to signaling priorities, there is another equally important consideration when it comes to thinking about resource provision and allocation. Resource provision also influences conditions for teacher motivation in two ways. ***First***, if you look back at Figure 1.4 in Chapter 1, you will see the Expectancy Model of Motivation. As you recall, this model assumes that a person is motivated to put forth an effort to attain a certain level of performance. This motivation is influenced by *expectancy*, or the probability that a given effort will lead to a desired level of performance. As a principal, you have the ability to influence and enhance the *expectancy* probability by providing adequate resources to enable teachers to do their jobs (Thomson, 1993). Put another way, teachers are more likely to be motivated to put forth an effort to attain a certain level of performance if they have the resources (time, materials, space, support, etc.) to do so. Stated in the negative, teachers with needs for professional and personal growth are less likely to be motivated to put forth an effort to attain a certain level of performance if inadequate resources are forthcoming (although I am constantly amazed at the stories I hear, particularly from elementary school teachers, of teachers digging into their own pockets to furnish basic supplies for their students!).

Second, the principal's role in resource provision would seem to have an influence on the critical psychological state of *experienced/felt meaningfulness of the work* noted in the Job Characteristics Model (see Fig. 1.5). Recall that *experienced/felt meaningfulness of the work* is the degree to which a person perceives and experiences his or her work as worthy, valuable, and important. This meaningfulness is influenced by *task significance*, or degree to which teachers' jobs have a substantial impact on the lives of other people. Although I have not come across this notion in the literature, it seems to me that to the extent the principal's role in providing resources signals to teachers the principal's priorities, to a similar extent this role indicates to teachers the significance that the principal attaches to their work. Priorities and significance are not quite the same. For instance, a principal might provide and allocate resources based on cogent instructional priorities, yet may not be a real advocate in the budget procurement process or may be overly frugal with discretionary funds. While priorities inform the principal's behaviors in providing and allocating resources, the lack of advocacy and/or stinginess with discretionary funds may indicate to teachers the significance the principal attaches to their work.

Thus, the principal's role in providing and allocating resources (1) signals to teachers what the principal thinks is important, (2) influences the degree to which teachers are motivated to put forth effort to attain a certain performance level, and (3) signals to teachers the degree to which the principal attaches significance to teachers' work. The types of resources under principals' control as well as strategies that principals can use to allocate and provide resources are discussed in the following section.

TYPES OF RESOURCES & STRATEGIES TO ALLOCATE

Inasmuch as we often do not think about how principals' behaviors in providing and allocating resources lends insight into principals' priorities for schools, perhaps we do not always consider the potpourri of resources at principals' disposal which, when provided, enhances the job conditions which result in teacher motivation. From my reading (see especially Blase & Blase, 1994; Blase & Kirby, 1992) and thoughts, there are no less than five different categories of resources at the principal's disposal:

- ***Organizational resources*** (time, teaching assignment, space, physical surroundings, etc.)
- ***Material/financial resources***
- ***Psychological and moral resources***
- ***Intellectual resources***
- ***Availability resources***

Each of these resources is discussed in the subsequent paragraphs.

Organizational resources. Already alluded to in the previous chapter, organizational resources include the precious resource of time, as well as space, physical surroundings, teaching assignments, etc.

Time is undoubtedly the resource that *no one* has enough of, particularly teachers. If money were not a problem (probably a hallucinatory consideration!) and I were a principal, teachers would teach one-half of the day and spend the other half day planning in teams for curricular and instructional improvement. This delusion aside, the principal as the allocator of time is absolutely duty-bound to protect teachers' instructional and planning time. Much as in Chapter 3 we discussed autonomy as *freedom from* and *freedom to,* I believe we can think about time as *time from* and *time to.* Simply put, teacher *time from* non-essential, non-instructional activities must be protected so that teachers have *time to* focus on the activities for which they are employed. Strategies to reduce teacher's *time from* might include:

- **Limiting teacher time spent in faculty meetings,** particularly when the purpose of the meeting is to disseminate information that could be disseminated through other media (memoranda, bulletins, e-mail, etc.)
- **Limiting teachers' out of class duty assignments.** This is a tough one to accomplish, particularly in elementary schools where teachers are with the same group of students all day, and in many secondary schools where there is a greater need for teachers to fulfill duty assignments. However, there are some things that principals can do to minimize time spent on these assignments, such as rotating assignments and times and not keeping a teacher on the same assignment all year (e.g., cafeteria or bus duty). Similarly, teachers' non-voluntary extracurricular duty assignments should be limited (teachers have families too, and if they want to spend all their time at school, they can become administrators!)
- **Reducing paperwork.** Is there any more to say?

- **Reducing classroom interruptions whenever possible.** In some cases, this is also a tough one. I look at this one from both a teacher's and an assistant principal's perspective. As a teacher, nothing made me angrier than having my class interrupted by an administrator getting a student out of my class to address a discipline problem, attendance matter, or other concern, particularly if the concern did not emanate from my class. As an assistant principal, I saw the other perspective: There are times when you just have to interrupt a teacher's class to see a student. The lesson to be learned here is to strike an appropriate balance between infringing on instructional time and necessarily interrupting a class. At a minimum, consider ways to reduce class interruptions *and* students' time out of class.

  There are other considerations when it comes to reducing classroom interruptions. Consider limiting and preferably forbidding fund-raising activities (candy sales, etc.), and delivery of non-emergency messages. In addition, severely curtail public address announcements and similar activities which infringe on instructional time.

- **Reducing the amount of time teachers spend on activities that could readily be done by paraprofessionals, teacher aides, or volunteers.** I hasten to add that these activities are important and certainly do not mean to diminish the contributions of our paraprofessionals, aides, and volunteers. On the contrary, our work as teachers and administrators would grind to a standstill were it not for the dedication and support of (as we say in Texas) "these fine folks." I would suggest that you find ways to have at least one aide or volunteer available to each grade level or department for the duration of each day to assist with such activities as paperwork, copying, typing, helping with classroom bulletin boards, etc., so that teachers can spend time on instructional concerns.

As I suggested earlier, once you have removed the *time from* barriers, it becomes important to work on the *time to* concerns.

Certainly, principals who remove *time from* barriers do so to provide teachers with *time to* teach, but there are other professional activities in which teachers should have *time to* engage. Some of these should be on teachers' own time, and some should encouraged and supported by the principal during the school day and year. Principals can provide teachers *time to* attend professional development meetings, observe colleagues teach, engage in curriculum writing, write instructional improvement grants, plan professional development activities, visit other schools to observe best practices, engage in administrative internship activities, participate in graduate education cohort groups, and so on. To be sure, principals must carefully balance the need for instructional continuity best accomplished by teachers teaching consistently against the need for teachers to grow professionally. Clearly, a teacher who misses 20 days during the course of the year for professionally related activities is missing too much time away from the classroom; on the other hand, teachers should be provided some *time to* engage in these activities. Therefore, there is an appropriate balance to be found.

Teaching assignments, although not necessarily thought of as resources, are another way that principals signal instructional priorities. In Chapter 3, I talked quite a bit about allocating teaching assignments, so I will not over dwell on this resource, except to offer a couple of suggestions for you to think about in allocating teaching assignments:

- Whether your school is organized by grade levels, departments, or is multi-disciplinary in nature, **strive to achieve a balance in assigning teaching duties**. Assess the teaching preferences of your staff regarding subject or grade level to be taught and time preferences for certain classes (if at all possible; and I understand that in the age of computerized master-scheduling it may not be) and try to incorporate individual preferences with the needs of the school. Avoid allowing teachers to be entrenched in the same teaching assignments year after year; variety across years and even within the year tends to reinvigorate the staff. In addition (and within the realm of reality, given collective bargaining agreements and the like), avoid establishing seniority as the predominant criterion for receiving the most favorable teaching assignments.

- In allocating teaching assignments, try to arrange schedules so that several teachers in the same grade level, on a subject area team, or on a multi-disciplinary team have **common planning periods**. In this way, you enhance the probability that teachers will have meaningful conversations about teaching and learning and can draw on their colleagues as resources.

Adequate space and physical surroundings are an extremely important resource over which the principal exercises influence. Each of us is more apt to work more productively in adequately spacious and pleasant, clean, and safe physical surroundings. It is difficult for teachers to work in classrooms that have broken windows, inadequate heat or air conditioning, poor ventilation, or students sitting on top of each other. In fact, from my experience, there are two people in each building whose support teachers and administrators absolutely must have. Pertinent to this discussion, that person is the **building custodian** (the other person is the principal's secretary). The relationship you build with the custodial staff will go a long way in determining the quality of the physical plant that is your building. In addition, teachers should be provided with adequate space in which to carry out non-classroom activities (such as team, grade level, or departmental office space).

Material/financial resources. At a minimum, this category of resources should include the instructional materials necessary for teachers to teach (including textbooks, workbooks, paper, copiers, projectors, etc.), orientations on where to find and how to use various pieces of equipment, financial support for teachers to supplement their instructional materials and supplies, and financial support for teachers' professional development activities. Again, a principal who provides adequate material and financial resources will enhance the probability that teachers' efforts will pay off in a desired level of performance (expectancy) and will indicate to the teaching staff that expectations for excellence are backed up with support to achieve excellence. Principals who wish to be effective material and financial resource providers should consider the following:

- **Anticipate and determine, prior to budget time, teachers' material and financial needs.** Elicit and incorporate **teacher input** in this process; base needs on your school's mission.
- **Be the advocate** for your building as the budget process unfolds. Always request what you need and back up your request with demonstrated needs and plans for using the resources. If you can demonstrate needs and plans for resource use, be reluctant to take no for an answer.
- **Seek other sources of funding** outside of the budget process. Consider business partnerships, teacher (or academic booster clubs), grant writing, and development activities. If your booster clubs or after-prom fund raisers can generate tens of thousands of dollars, there are resources to be had.
- **Assess needs on a continuous basis.** Reallocate resources as necessary and in sync with the school's mission.

Psychological and moral resources. When I mention psychological and moral resources, I am thinking about the support that principals provide teachers when teachers address student instructional or behavioral concerns, parental concerns, or concerns in which teachers depend on the principal for moral support (including the support of the principal for teachers to take risks; see the next section on innovation). Teachers absolutely depend on our unqualified support (at least publicly) when it comes to backing them up in instructional matters, student discipline matters, and conflicts with parents. Principals who effectively provide psychological and moral support to teachers do so by:

- ***In cases where teachers have followed established policies and have acted in good faith,* supporting publicly**, and if necessary, **counseling and/or reprimanding privately** (this is admittedly tough to do at times; just remember, *many of us* have made mistakes and were bailed out by a supportive principal). When teachers do not follow policies and do not act in good faith and students suffer as a result, the matter becomes different. Even so, principals are obligated to keep teachers informed and teachers are obligated to keep themselves informed of policy changes and what constitutes acting in "good faith."

- **Conveying to teachers expectations for handling the "people" matters**, whether the people are students, parents, or colleagues and then **making sure that we provide teachers with the "people skill" training** to live up to these expectations. Moreover, we need to listen, offer advice, and help teachers solve their student discipline problems (Blase & Kirby, 1992) on a one-to-one basis.
- **Being highly visible in the building.**
- **Being available to participate in teacher/student, teacher/parent, or teacher/student/parent conferences**, particularly for early career teachers or for conferences that have the possibility of getting out of hand.
- **Establishing student codes of conduct**, collaborating with building and district staff to set clear expectations for student behavior, providing teacher staff development with regard to the student code, and applying the code uniformly.
- **Providing opportunities for teachers and parents to meet** early in the school year BEFORE problems arise. In fact, I would encourage your teachers to call all of their students' parents during the first two weeks of school. Let's face it, when the school calls, it usually means trouble; we must break away from this and can do so. For example, I was fortunate enough to have a grade level counselor, Carolyn Boyce, and two in-building administrative interns, Bobby Morris and Donna Grant, as part of our grade level team. During my second and third years at Westfield High School, we contacted (at least once during the year, by phone the first year and by mail the second year) each parent of the Class of 1995 (approximately 650 students) and invited them to a bi-weekly parent meeting. At these meetings (which lasted one hour), we discussed issues of importance to the

class and to the parents and gave them tours of our career and college guidance center. The parental support we garnered from these meetings was outstanding. The amount of parental support you can generate from an activity like this, where no adversarial relationship exists, is well worth the tremendous amount of time and effort necessary to pull it off. I highly recommend similar activities to your teachers; calling parents can be accomplished by teachers within two weeks.

Intellectual resources. Intellectual resources include those resources necessary to contribute to teachers' instructional effectiveness and professional growth. We extensively discussed this matter in the previous chapter (providing intellectually stimulating work roles).

Availability resources. For lack of a better term, I have coined availability resources as the principal's willingness to be available to staff to address their concerns. Principals know that teachers expect them to be there; as the leader of their building, principals have an obligation to do so. We all have had, either as a teacher or an administrator, early morning or late evening conversations with teaching or administrative colleagues about concerns very real to us. It should come as no surprise that the principal's role in this resource area includes getting to school early and staying late (an occupational reality), having an open-door policy, attending school functions, and generally being highly visible. For those of you who are thinking about becoming a principal, you might as well expect this to be a reality!

SUPPORTING INNOVATION

Science teacher (to principal): Wow! Last night I was surfing the net and I came across a high school homepage on the web which had descriptions and pictures of their school's winning science fair projects. If we only had a computer with ISDN lines and a connection to the net, I could project these descriptions to a screen and really get my kiddos fired up about the district science fair competition! We could even e-mail the teachers and students and find out how they did it!

Principal A (to the teacher): That sounds great. Too bad we can't get any resources to do this

Principal B (to the same teacher): Wow! Let's see what we can do to get this going!

Although it is entirely possible that this teacher could not get support for this innovation, which principal would you rather work for?

We discussed in Chapter 3 that principals create conditions for teacher motivation in part by designing jobs which enable teachers to utilize a variety of skills and perform complete rather than isolated tasks. Further, to enhance skill variety and task identity, and thus create conditions for teachers to experience that their work is meaningful, teacher work activities must be intellectually stimulating and challenging. As part of designing jobs that are intellectually stimulating and challenging (and to come up with better ways to improve schooling), the principal's role necessarily includes supporting meaningful innovation as a means to school improvement.

What exactly is innovation? It seems to have something to do with change, but is it entirely change? Not being exactly sure, I looked up the word "innovation" in the Second College Edition of the *American Heritage Dictionary* (1982, p. 663) and found innovation defined as "the act of innovating." Innovate is previously defined as "to begin or introduce something new; be creative." Then I thought about what the word "new" means, because in the education profession we tend to think of things as new when they are really not new and jump on the latest bandwagon, only to discover that we have been down that road before. "New" is defined in 12 distinct ways in the same dictionary (p. 839); the following four definitions seem to be most applicable to our discussion:

- Having existed or been made for only a short time; recent . . .
- Just found, discovered, or learned. . .
- Unfamiliar; novel . . .
- Modern, current.

Why this emphasis on words and definitions? I think, in this case, these words are important because it helps signal to the principal the role he or she must play in not only supporting innovation, but also recognizing him or herself what innovation really is. For example, definitions (a), (b), and (d) above suggest several roles that the principal can play to support new ideas and ways of doing things to improve the school. In order to keep current with and to keep staff current with ideas and methods that are recent or newly discovered, the principal should:

- **Be a voracious reader, inquirer, and listener**. *Reading* in and out of our respective fields is how we keep up with the latest research and best practice to improve schools. Of course, we cannot be experts in everything: in addition to reading, we need to be *inquiring* of our colleagues (particularly teachers) in their respective fields and *listening* to them about the ideas and practices they have come across in their professional development.
- In addition to reading, inquiring, and listening, principals and teachers need to become more capable **consumers of research** and be able to distinguish quality research from suspect research (see the volume in *The School Leadership Library* on "Measurement and Evaluation"). I'm reminded of a story told by one of my students in the research class I teach at East Texas State University. She told me that she was sitting in her principal's office when a salesperson came in to sell the principal some type of computerized instructional program. The salesperson claimed that students who use this program actually numerically increased the number of neurons in their brains! Her principal, obviously a capable consumer of research, questioned the salesperson on the research base to support the claim. To make a long story short, the principal did not purchase the program. The point is that being a capable consumer of research does not require a graduate degree in educational psychology or statistics.

- Not only encourage your teachers to be voracious readers, inquirers, and listeners, but **provide them with the opportunities and the means** to do so. We have discussed many strategies in earlier chapters, but there are other things principals can do to encourage and provide opportunities. Each building should have a professional reading area; literature can be provided either by the school or by staff members who undoubtedly subscribe to a wide variety of professional journals. In addition, take some of the staff development days built into your calendar for which you might otherwise hire an "expert" to come in and preach and turn them into discussion seminars where teachers actually have a chance to talk to each other about what they have read and tried, how they have succeeded or failed, and why. Participate in these seminars!
- When you come across a professional development opportunity (reading, attending a conference, visiting another school, etc.), drop an article or note in a teacher's box and **suggest the opportunity to participate** to the teacher. Moreover, ask the teacher if there is anything you could do to facilitate his or her participation (such as cover a class, provide registration fees, etc.).
- **Encourage** teachers to initiate well conceived **pilot projects, support** those efforts, and **celebrate** those who participate. Many of your innovations start in a corner of the building, perhaps with a teacher, or among a grade level or subject area team. The more pilot projects that you have going in your building, the more likely one of them is to succeed.

Definition (c) of "new" suggests that innovation is to begin to introduce something that is unfamiliar or novel. The unfamiliar or novel is uncomfortable for a lot of reasons, not the least of which is that it becomes more challenging and difficult (at least initially) to do things in unfamiliar ways. In addition, doing things differently affects each person involved in the change; therefore, the first thing each person asks him or herself is "how is the innovation/unfamiliar/change going to affect me personally?" Moreover, there are risks involved in introducing an innovation. These risks include the fear of failure; the fear of taking blame for failure, regardless of the part one plays in the innovation; the fear of risking personal and professional credibility; the fear of losing support of the staff; and the fear of upsetting the status quo.

In this regard, these are some things that principals can do to alleviate the psychological barriers to innovation and create, as Peters (1988, p. 275) puts it, "a corporate capacity for innovation." Please consider the following and at the same time reflect on how this currently applies and can apply to your professional work:

- **Model innovation on your part**. Constantly seek better ways of doing things, whether it be improving office procedures, revamping the tardy policy, improving the way parent/teacher conferences are handled, or some other new activity. Modeling behaviors, such as respecting and being receptive to new ideas, are probably the most powerful signals you can send to your staff that you believe in looking for ways to improve your practice and that you are not afraid to take a risk or to fail.
- Particularly for planned, large scale innovations (which are probably more appropriately termed change), **understand theories and processes of change** (see the end of the chapter for suggested readings). In this way, your chances for implementing planned innovations will be enhanced.
- **Create a culture and climate** in which **teachers' are respected and valued** for having ideas (no matter how wacky!), where there is an atmosphere of **trust**, where there is encouragement to take **risks**, where there is **freedom to fail**, and where there is **freedom from criticism for failing**. You've no doubt read this before, so there are only a couple of things I'd like to add. ***First***, freedom to fail does not mean freedom to be slipshod or sloppy (Peters, 1988). It just means that not every innovation is going to succeed. Innovations should be *well conceived, in tune with the school's mission and core*

values (the "what is good" from Sergiovanni, 1992), must be *legal,* must be *ethical,* and *cannot harm students or interfere with their learning.* When these criteria are met, teachers who try innovations should be hailed, and not castigated, if the innovation fails. ***Second,*** a climate in which teachers' are respected and valued for having ideas means just that . . . *all teachers are respected and valued for having ideas.* Now, we know that some ideas are better than others, and that some ideas are just not good (and it's often hard to value and respect those who come up with bad ideas, especially continually). Moreover, we know that on each teaching staff are at least two devil's advocates who are skeptical of every idea that comes down the pike. *Put these folks to work and listen to them!* Healthy and informed dissent is important (Yukl, 1989), particularly in our profession where dissent from the popular norm is often discouraged, and even at times vilified. Therefore, this culture of respect also consists of respect for the dissenters, because they might just have a better idea.

- Constantly look at other schools which are successful and see how they are doing it. When you come across another school which has a successful innovation, **send a team of teachers** to observe the innovation. Don't send yourself. You might already be sold on the innovation, so there's not nearly as much need for you to go as there is for a team of teachers to go. When you send this team, also send one of your dissenters! Upon their return from the site visit, arrange for the team to present their findings to those staff members who will be ultimately affected by the change.
- **Create structures for innovation**. Most successful innovations start as small (Peters, 1988) pilot projects and thus are started by a few people who have an idea of how to do things better. Very few ideas, let alone good ones, come out of large meetings (particularly in universities and schools). Accordingly, principals can create innovation structures by encouraging the formation of small, informal, and often cross-

disciplinary teams to think about and implement better ways of doing things in schools. I believe that the greater the number of small teams, the greater the number of good ideas you'll have.

- **Run interference for the innovators**. Those of you who are football fans (and old enough) probably remember the University of Southern California teams of the late 1960s and 1970s which produced several Heisman Trophy running backs. I remember watching these teams play; the Trojans' favorite play during this era was called "Student Body Right." On this play, the quarterback would hand the ball to the running back and the entire offensive line would go to the right and clear the way for the ball carrier. In the same manner, the principal runs interference for the innovators in the building by encouraging and supporting innovation, scrounging together resources for the project, obtaining waivers from unnecessary rules and regulations, celebrating the innovators and the project, and institutionalizing the innovation if it is successful.

To conclude this section, perhaps the principal's two most important behaviors are the first and last ones that I have just addressed: *Modeling* and *running interference* for the innovators on your staff. The innovators are there, the ideas are there. They are just looking for the opportunity to happen.

SUMMARY

In this chapter we examined the principal's role in providing resources and supporting innovation. We first noted that the principal's role as resource provider and allocator lends insight as to what the principal values and thinks is important in the school. We also pointed out that the principal's role in providing adequate resources to teachers enhances conditions which can result in teacher motivation in two ways: (1) The adequate provision of resources enhances the probability that a teacher's effort will result in a desired performance level (*expectancy*) and (2) the provision of resources signals to the staff the significance that the principal attaches to the staff's work. To that end, we noted five categories of resources at the principals disposal (organizational, material/financial, psychological/moral, intellectual, and availability) and strategies that principals can consider to more effectively provide and allocate these resources.

In the second part of this chapter, we discussed the principal's role in supporting innovation on the part of the instructional staff. We argued that the principal's role in supporting innovation complements his or her behavior in providing job conditions that are challenging and intellectually stimulating. We began by examining the words "innovation" and "new." Based on this examination, we noted a collection of strategies and behaviors a principal can utilize to support well conceived, mission- and value-oriented, legal, and ethical innovations. In concluding, we posited that the two most important principal behaviors in supporting innovation were to model innovation and to remove barriers (run interference) to innovation.

In thinking about why I chose to devote this chapter to these two topics, I came to the conclusion that I did so because it seems that we hear two recurring and related themes on the landscape. The first is that we must change much of what we do in public education if we are going to prepare students to flourish in the next century. The second theme seems to be that although we must change, we are not going to have any more resources to do so, and we may have less. There is probably more than a shred of truth in each theme; this is why the leadership of the building principal, in bringing about meaningful change (not just for the sake of changing) and providing and allocating a seemingly fixed amount of resources to do so, is so vitally important. This leadership challenge might be the greatest challenge to face the principal in the near future.

ACTION PLAN

- Assess your building budgeting process in light of your school's mission. Are fiscal resources targeted toward what is really important? Is the staff involved in the process?

- Assess your staff's perception of the quality and accessibility of the "intangible" resources, i.e., psychological and moral, intellectual, and availability resources. Do the staff feel supported? If not, why not, and how can you increase staff perceptions of support? Are you available to the extent that you need to be?
- Find three ways to immediately remove teachers' *time from* barriers so that teachers may have more *time to* devote to instructional and professional development concerns. In at least one way think about how you can more effectively utilize support personnel to accomplish this. Track the degree to which teacher *time from* is converted into *time to*.
- Immediately find three innovative projects in your building and think about ways you can support these projects. If there are not three occurring, get them started.
- Immediately examine your building's organization and determine if this organization facilitates innovation, planning, and teachers talking to each other. If your current organizational structure does not, find ways to change it.
- Begin to examine best practices at successful schools in your locale, particularly in regard to practices which can use improvement in your building. Send teams of your staff to visit these schools and to report to the faculty on these practices.

SUGGESTED READINGS

Blase, J., & Blase, J.R. (1994). *Empowering teachers: What successful principals do.* Thousand Oaks, CA: Corwin Press. (See especially Chapter 4 titled "A Cornucopia of Supportive Resources.")

Brewer, E.W., Achilles, C.M., & Fuhriman, J.R. (1995). *Finding funding: Grantwriting and project management from start to finish* (2nd ed.). Thousand Oaks, CA: Corwin Press. (Written for school administrators, this book includes addresses and phone numbers for funding agencies and is organized around three themes: (1) Exploring the grants world, (2) Writing grant proposals, and (3) Implementing, operating, and terminating a project.)

Owens, R.G. (1991). *Organizational behavior in education* (4th ed.). Boston: Allyn & Bacon. (See especially Chapter 8 titled "Organizational Change".)

Peters, T. (1988). *Thriving on chaos*. New York: Alfred A. Knopf, Inc. (See especially Chapter 3 titled "Pursuing Fast-Paced Innovation.")

Yukl, G.A. (1989). *Leadership in organizations* (2nd ed.). Englewood Cliffs, NJ: Prentice-Hall. (See especially Chapter 10 titled "Charismatic and Transformational Leadership" as it relates to innovation.)

5

PROVIDING MENTORSHIP

Mentor: "A wise and trusted counselor and teacher"
(*American Heritage Dictionary*, 1982, p. 786)

The words to the definition of mentor are indeed powerful, particularly when we consider the principal's role in providing mentorship to the teaching staff. According to this definition, the principal as mentor should possess the following four characteristics (the subsequent descriptions are paraphrased from the *American Heritage Dictionary*, 1982):

- **Wisdom**, including knowledge, common sense, and understanding
- **Trustworthiness**, or to be a person of confidence, integrity, ability, and character
- **Counsel**, including advice, guidance, and a plan of action
- **Teaching**, including providing knowledge and causing to learn by experience.

In addition, several words synonymous with mentor (Rodale, 1978) shed greater light as to exactly what the principal's role in mentorship is: Counselor, advisor, guide, coach, teacher, educator, and wise person. Arguably implicit in the roles of advisor, coach, teacher, and educator is the role of providing feedback.

Accordingly, although I have titled this chapter "Providing Mentorship," I refer to mentorship as the principal's role in providing guidance, coaching, and feedback to teaching staff. After some discussion as to why mentorship is important, we will examine how the principal, operating in the role of mentor, can create conditions for teacher motivation.

PERSPECTIVES

FEEDBACK

Just above, we operationally defined mentorship as providing guidance, coaching, and feedback. However, to put mentorship in perspective, it is probably more effective to *think* about our definition in reverse: providing feedback, coaching, and guidance. When we first examined the Job Characteristics Model (see Fig. 1.5), we noted that one of the critical psychological states that can lead to enhanced teacher motivation is *knowledge of the actual results of work activities*, or the extent to which the individual continuously knows and understands the effectiveness of his or her job performance (Hackman & Oldham, 1976). This critical psychological state is influenced by the core job characteristic of *feedback*, or "the degree to which carrying out the work activities required by the job results in the individual obtaining direct and clear information about the effectiveness of his or her performance" (p. 258).

Intuitively, when we think about feedback, we think about feedback provided by or provided to a supervisor, colleague, or subordinate. Please notice that Hackman & Oldham's (1976) definition of feedback suggests that feedback is not provided by a *person*, but rather is provided by the *work activities* of the job itself (Hoy & Miskel, 1991, 1996). For example, a teacher might receive feedback on his or her teaching performance through a state-mandated teacher appraisal instrument, for which the evaluator might be a principal. This exemplifies *person-oriented* feedback. In contrast, a teacher might receive feedback on his or her teaching performance by observing a student's behavior improve after changing that student's seating assignment. This exemplifies *job-oriented* feedback. Perhaps a better example might come from comparing the sports of gymnastics and golf. In competitive gymnastics, feedback on an individual's performance is provided by a panel of judges who assign a score for each routine; this feedback is *person-oriented*. In golf (which is always competitive!), feedback on an individual's performance is provided by the shot itself (for example, did the shot land on the green or in the water?); this feedback is *job-oriented*.

Why is this distinction important, particularly in this era of accountability when it is important to quantify how well teachers teach and students learn? To be sure, this accountability movement is not going to disappear anytime soon and principals will probably evaluate teachers in some way for the foreseeable future. In fact, the principal must be an important source of providing feedback to teachers (Thomson, 1993). The distinction is nonetheless important because it suggests that the degree to which the *job itself* is designed to provide feedback, to that degree the job itself can be a source of motivation to teachers.

COACHING AND GUIDANCE

One of the best teaching lessons I've ever witnessed provides an excellent example of what coaching and guidance entails. The lesson was provided by Emory Bellard, who was the football coach at Westfield High School during my tenure as an assistant principal. For those of you not familiar with football, or not from Texas, Emory Bellard is an example of a "living legend." Emory invented the "Wishbone" offense while an assistant coach at the University of Texas and parlayed this innovation into successful head coaching tenures at Texas A&M University and Mississippi State University. He then came out of an early retirement to successfully coach high school football at Westfield until his second retirement in 1993.

Emory was asked to be part of the beginning-of-school inservice activity and to give a demonstration lesson on the "Wishbone" offense to illustrate the similarities between classroom teaching and on-the-field coaching (which in reality are the same), and now by analogy, the principal's role as a coach and guide. For 15–20 minutes, Emory held the 160–170 person faculty in rapt attention (remember, teachers are often the toughest audience) as he taught the technical vocabulary and intricacies of the wishbone offense. Additionally, by showing film from practice sessions, Emory illustrated the expectations for each player in the offense, demonstrated how each player had to function to fulfill his expectations, and provided guidance as to how each player could more effectively fulfill his expectations to make the "Wishbone" successful. At the end of the lesson, Emory received a well deserved, rousing, and standing ovation from the entire faculty (some of whom were skeptical at the outset).

What did this seemingly innocuous lesson demonstrate? To me, at least, it demonstrated what is entailed by providing coaching and guidance to students, players, or in our case, teachers. In this lesson, Emory clearly illustrated the expectations of each player at each position, demonstrated the function of each player, and provided guidance as to how each player could fulfill expectations. By analogy, principals as coaches and guides convey clear expectations for staff performance, model these expectations in their daily work, and are there to provide the guidance necessary to assist teachers in fulfilling expectations. (Perhaps the difference in this analogy is that expectations for high school players tend to be set by coaches, whereas expectations for teachers might be set more collaboratively.)

In the Expectancy Model of Motivation (see Fig. 1.4), we noted that the degree to which individuals are motivated is influenced by *expectancy*, or the probability that a given effort will lead to a desired performance level. Stated differently, if individuals believe that their efforts will lead to a desired performance level, then they are more likely to be motivated to exert the necessary effort. This expectancy probability has important implications for the principal's role as coach and guide. To enhance teacher expectancy, the principal should do several things. ***First***, the principal should set (either collaboratively with teachers, by him or herself, or empower the teacher to set) clear *expectations* for desired performance and the effort necessary to achieve this performance level. ***Second***, the principal should clarify and communicate these expectations for teacher performance, individually and collectively, on a consistent basis. ***Third***, the principal should convey these expectations to staff by modeling these expectations in his or her work activities (to be discussed more fully in Chapter 7). ***Fourth*** (as discussed extensively in the last chapter), the principal should provide the resources for teachers to achieve a desired performance level for their expended effort. ***Fifth***, the principal should provide guidance for teachers to enhance the expectancy probability. ***Finally***, when it becomes necessary and after a good faith effort to remediate, principals should have the courage to take corrective action (including removal) for teachers who just are not able to attain expectations.

The concept of expectations has obviously received a great deal of attention in the preceding paragraphs. Without question, each of us feels more comfortable in our work if we know what is expected of us. Unclear or ambiguous role expectations of teachers (i.e., role ambiguity) place teachers in a position of trying to guess what the principal expects in terms of performance. This role ambiguity among teachers has been found to be consistently related in a negative way to teacher satisfaction (i.e., the greater the ambiguity, the less the satisfaction) (Thompson, 1994). Thus, teachers, while desiring autonomy in carrying out daily activities, need to clearly know what is expected of them.

In addition, principals must not only set (or help to set, or allow teachers to set) expectations, but must also continuously communicate and clarify these expectations. According to Yukl (1989), clarifying includes communicating plans, policies, and expectations to staff as well as providing necessary instruction in how to meet these expectations. Clarifying expectations, while not motivational in nature (motivation aims to energize behavior), serves to guide and orient behavior by making expectations clear.

Finally, above and beyond setting, communicating, and clarifying expectations for performance, the principal's role in coaching and guidance must include providing the guidance necessary for teachers to meet performance expectations. Setting, communicating, and clarifying expectations, without providing guidance to meet these expectations (whether the guidance is in the form of individual or group staff development, peer mentorship, growth plans, etc.), is as harmful to teachers as being the victims of unclear expectations. Therefore, the next section will discuss means for principals to enhance their role in coaching and guidance.

COACHING AND GUIDANCE

EXPECTATIONS AND GOAL SETTING

Expectations. Expectations and goals are not the same, but are probably similar enough to be discussed in the same context.

Both are important, however, in creating conditions for teacher motivation. Expectations are demands and obligations placed on an individual (Hoy & Miskel, 1996); these demands and obligations may be placed on an individual by the organization, by a member of the organization (e.g., a superintendent, principal, teacher), or by the individual him or herself. Goals, too, can be individual or organizational. Individually speaking, goals constitute what individuals intentionally and consciously attempt to achieve; organizationally speaking, goals are desired outcomes which guide the behavior of an organization (Hoy & Miskel, 1996). Although substantial congruence between individual and organizational expectations and goals is desirable (particularly in schools), the focus of our discussion will be on expectations and goals as vehicles for energizing individual behavior.

Perhaps an example is necessary to differentiate between expectations and goals. Speaking as a former administrator and knowing how most principals behave, I'm sure that you are subject to an organizational expectation that you arrive at school not later than a certain time, say 7:00 a.m. Because early morning hours are very conducive to catching up on paperwork and similar work, you may have a self-imposed expectation that you arrive at school between 6:00 and 6:15 a.m. In order to meet this individual expectation, you have to set at least four goals. First, you have to get up between 5:00 and 5:15 a.m. Second, you have to make sure you get six or seven hours of sleep, meaning you have to get to bed by 10:00 or 10:15 p.m. the night before (if you don't have extracurricular activity duty!). Third, you have to make sure family and personal obligations are taken care of prior to 10:00 p.m. the night before. And fourth, you have to make sure all necessary school obligations are taken care of before you leave school the previous day so that you can devote time and attention to whatever needs to be addressed the next morning at school. Mundane goals, to be sure, but goals nonetheless!

This example illustrates several things. ***First***, expectations are important to us as we set individual goals. Whether you expect to obtain a graduate degree down the line, expect a level of performance from yourself, or expect a certain level of performance from your teaching staff, these expectations help you and others set individual goals. ***Second,*** goals to operationalize and even set parameters for our expectations. For example, those of you who have written a thesis or dissertation certainly imposed that expectation on yourself; by setting goals (such as a time frame for the completion of each chapter), you operationally defined your expectation and set parameters for achieving your expectation. ***Third,*** individual goals energize behavior. In our example above, your behavior is motivated and energized by setting these four goals to meet your expectation of arriving at school in enough time to catch up on paperwork (probably why principals always seem to feel as if they're in a hurry!). ***Fourth,*** the specificity of the goals in the example motivated you to achieve your self-imposed expectation of arriving early to school.

Clearly, teachers in our schools are subject to organizational, supervisory, collegial, and individual expectations. Organizationally, teachers are expected to be competent in the technical core of teaching (subject matter expertise, teaching methods, lesson planning, etc.). Principals expect teachers to go beyond technical competence; teachers are expected to be professional in their work, punctual, motivated (*and* motivators of students), accountable for student performance, and so on. Teachers have certain expectations of their colleagues; for example, teachers expect colleagues to "pull their weight" in team activities, expect their colleagues to be competent technically, and expect collegial support in important matters. Finally, teachers have certain self-imposed expectations (ideally, to be the "best teachers that they can be").

Thus, the principal's role in setting, conveying, and clarifying expectations for teachers has an organizational and individual component. Regardless of the type, the principal needs to be aware of several things in this area:

- Set and convey expectations that are **clear and unambiguous**. For example, whether conveying an expectation to the entire staff or to an individual teacher, the expectation of "This year, we expect student punctuality to class to improve significantly" is not nearly as clear as "This year, we will reduce by one-half the number of tardies in our building."

- Set and convey expectations that are **high, yet attainable**. This is fairly congruent with our discussion in Chapter 3 on the skill/challenge balance (and even the effective schools research). Expectations that are easy to attain will not challenge teachers and will result in boredom and diminished motivation. Expectations that are clearly unattainable can stifle motivation.
- **Involve staff** in setting expectations for organizational and individual performance. Organizationally, by involving staff, you might very well get an idea of what is doable and what is unrealistic, given your current organizational context. Intuitively, by involving staff, you would expect to gain greater commitment to the expectations. In addition, I think it is important to meet with individual staff, be it formally or informally, to set individual expectations for performance and to clarify any concerns that individual teachers might have.
- **Consistently and frequently** articulate and clarify expectations for individual and organizational performance. From experience, the most powerful means to do this is *individually and informally*. While it is important to do this with the whole staff from time to time, a simple, individual, and informal "what are you currently doing to improve instruction in your classroom?" just as clearly articulates an expectation. Moreover, it signals to teachers that the expectation is not hollow.
- **Articulate your confidence** in the staff and individual teachers to attain expectations. This confidence is not something that you can fake; your staff will know quickly—typically by your actions—whether you believe they are capable of attaining performance expectations.
- **Be up-front** about the effort that is going to be required by the *entire staff* or the *individual* to attain these expectations. Avoid sugarcoating your expectations by implying that little additional effort will be necessary to attain them. If attaining an individual expectation requires additional professional development for a teacher, let the teacher know; then provide the support

necessary for that teacher to participate in that development.

- **Recognize and celebrate** individual and organizational attainment of expectations (See Chapter 6).
- **Have in place legal, defensible, and humane policies and procedures** to remove teachers who are ultimately unable to attain expectations.

Goals. As we noted earlier, expectations and goals are quite similar in one respect, yet different in another. Expectations are other- or self-imposed demands or obligations placed on an individual, while goals are what individuals consciously and intentionally attempt to achieve (Hoy & Miskel, 1996). In a sense, expectations define roles in an organization and are the "official blueprint" (p. 36) for action; goals might be thought of as intermediary and purposive guides for individual action within the organization.

Individual goal setting is an important source of motivation. In fact, the basic tenet of goal setting theory (Hoy & Miskel, 1996) is that the major force motivating an individual's work behavior is that person's attempt to attain a goal. In their evaluation of goal setting theory, Hoy and Miskel (1996; drawing on the work of Locke & Latham, 1990; see also Yukl, 1989) cite the following generalizations which enjoy support across time, activities, and situations:

- Goals which are difficult *and* accepted, as opposed to easy goals, result in higher performance levels.
- Higher performance levels result from goals which are specific and formidable as opposed to goals which are ambiguous and non-verifiable.
- Regardless of the origin of goals (set by others, set collaboratively, or set by self), goals are powerful motivators.

This last generalization is important to the principal's role as mentor. Although it intuitively seems that collaboratively- or self-set goals would foster greater goal commitment and performance, recent research evidence fails to support this claim (Hoy & Miskel, 1996). There are, I think, two practical applications from this last generalization. ***First***, even though there seems to be no difference in goal commitment and job performance based on goal origin, it is probably better practice for principals to collaboratively set many individual goals with teachers or to have teachers formulate some individual goals. ***Second***, this generalization suggests that principals can play a powerful role in creating conditions for motivating individuals through their goal setting behavior. Specifically, there are situations in which it is not only appropriate, but obligatory, for principals to set goals for individual staff; these situations might include setting goals for teachers' instructional behaviors, classroom management techniques, professional development activities, and so on. The challenge for the principal, I believe, comes in striking a balance between the origin of goals.

What then, are the other practical applications of goal setting as a major source of individual motivation? Again, drawing on the excellent work of Hoy & Miskel (1996), these applications and examples are offered:

- **Goals should relate and contribute to organizational and individual expectations and goals**.
- The goal to be achieved should be **difficult, but attainable**. In addition, goals should be based on the individual's level of expertise, which is constantly changing. For example, goals for an early career teacher will be qualitatively different from those for a master teacher.
- As a corollary to difficult and attainable goals, goals should be **realistic in number and the time** necessary to attain the goals. Again, these parameters of realism will depend on the individual to whom the goal applies. In some cases, one goal with a great deal of time to achieve it is enough. In other cases, multiple goals with varying time parameters are appropriate.
- The individual goal should be **specific and clear**, i.e., easily communicated and understandable. For example, a principal's goal to "spend more time out of the office and in classrooms" is not as specific and clear as a principal's goal to "spend at least one hour per day informally visiting classrooms." The shorter the wording of the goal, the more likely it is to be clear. American

theatrical producer David Belasco once said, "If you can't get your idea on the back of my calling card, you don't have a clear idea." This bit of advice is excellent for goal setting.

- Although we have noted that recent research suggests there is no difference in goal commitment and performance level based on goal origin, to be effective motivators **goals must be accepted** by those setting the goals, particularly by the individual who will be primarily responsible for attaining the goals. For example, if you as a principal set for a teacher the goal of reducing the number of discipline referrals coming to the office, and this goal is neither acceptable to or realistically attained by the teacher, this goal is quite unlikely to be attained. Again, the challenge for you as principal is to determine the type of goal being set and how to engender goal acceptance. Some goals, in fact, will need to be negotiated.
- If multiple goals are being set, **goals should be prioritized** according to importance. For instance, you and one of your master teachers might agree on the following two goals for the teacher: (1) To devote two hours per week to peer coaching teacher colleagues, and (2) to devote three hours per month to curriculum development. If both goals require that time spent on these activities come out of the school day, these goals might have to be prioritized.
- **Goal attainment should be capable of being evaluated**, either quantitatively or qualitatively. This follows from goal clarity and specificity. For example, it is far easier for the principal to evaluate attainment of his or her goal to "spend at least one hour per day informally visiting classrooms" than the general goal of spending "more time out of the office and in classrooms." Moreover, it is important to evaluate the qualitative aspects of goal attainment. In this example, qualitative aspects of attaining this goal include the less perceptible or measurable effects of informal classroom visits on teachers, students, and self. These less measurable

effects might include building trust with teachers and students, increased feelings of efficacy on the part of teachers, and so on.

Of course, there is one major assumption which underlies goal setting and is crucial to its success. This assumption is that a wide array of resources is available to assist staff members in attaining goals. In addition to the resources discussed in Chapter 4 (i.e., organizational, material/financial, moral and psychological, intellectual, and availability), an additional resource which must be available to teachers is the guidance displayed on the part of the principal. This guidance is the subject of the next section.

GUIDANCE

When I think about the principal's role in guiding, I tend to think about what a guide is. As a youngster, I was fortunate enough to visit the Chicago Museum of Science and Industry. Part of the visit included a guided tour of the Museum. As part of her task, the tour guide led the tour group throughout the mammoth Museum. From time to time, she directed our attention to exhibits of particular significance (I vividly remember seeing the command module from the Saturn V rockets used in the Apollo space missions). And throughout the tour, our guide would answer questions or advise us on the finer points of exhibits. However, the guide did not take the tour for us, we experienced the tour with the assistance of the guide.

As another part of guidance, I think back just three or four years ago to the time that I was in the midst of writing my doctoral dissertation. I was fortunate to have dissertation committee co-chairs who also played the role of guides (in fact, a dissertation is not unlike a tour in many respects!) as the process unfolded. Much the same as the tour guide on my trip through the museum, my co-chairs provided leadership in helping me to select a topic, to set and meet deadlines, and to use the right statistical tools; provided direction in helping me to select courses, to formulate my research problem, and to survey the pertinent literature (e.g., "have you read this article?" or "you need to take this class"); and certainly provided pertinent advice throughout the whole process. Yet, they did not write the dissertation; with the guidance of my committee, I wrote it.

Both of these examples of guidance provide a useful way to think about the role of the principal as a guide (or even mentor). In each of these examples, the guides provided leadership, direction, and advice, while the individuals experienced the tour. Much the same, the principal as guide must provide leadership, direction, and advice in order for the organization and teachers in the organization to attain their goals; yet, each teacher in the organization experiences the goal attainment process.

Moreover, these examples illustrate each of the four characteristics of mentorship noted on the first page of this chapter, namely, *wisdom*, *trustworthiness*, *counsel*, and *teaching*. In each example, the "tour guides" possessed the knowledge and understanding necessary to guide the tour; the character, integrity, confidence, and ability to be trusted; the advice and guidance to make the tour more meaningful; and the knowledge and means for the tour takers to learn by and from the experience of the tour. It is around these four characteristics of mentorship that I would like to discuss the principal's role as guide.

Wisdom. While principals are not and cannot be specialists in every subject area or grade level, there is certain knowledge and understanding that principals must possess to be effective guides. At a minimum, these certain knowledges and understandings include:

- **Understanding and remembering teachers' challenges and understanding teachers' developmental needs**. These understandings imply that principals should spend ample time in classrooms to gauge challenges and developmental needs.
- Knowledge of **various supervision options** (for an excellent, yet concise discussion of these options, see Sergiovanni, 1991, Chapter 14) and understanding of the type of supervision option which best meets teachers' **needs**.
- Knowledge and understanding of **what constitutes effective teaching** for varying types of instructional methods (direct, cooperative, inductive, etc.).

- Knowledge and understanding of **one's own limitations** in guiding teachers (we all have them); by application, knowledge and understanding of where to direct teachers for assistance in goal attainment.

Trustworthiness. While this characteristic will be developed more fully in Chapter 7, we have noted that this trait includes ability, integrity, character, and confidence. Many principals are obligated by state mandate or district policy to evaluate teachers for tenure, merit pay increases, or simple renewal of a probationary contract, and at the same time are expected to serve as mentors for teachers. While there is undoubtedly a conflict in these roles, principals who are trustworthy are far more able to function in these dual roles than those who are not. Simply put, when it comes to mentoring and guiding, teachers must be able to trust not only the knowledge of principals, but must especially be able to trust the motives of principals. Clearly, the primary motive of the principal in mentoring should be for teachers' professional development and the attainment of individual and organizational goals. Integrity suggests that when a principal says that he or she is going to do something to assist the teacher, then the principal is going to do it.

Frase (1992) suggests several strategies that principals can use to build and maintain trust with teachers. Although these suggestions are offered in the context of assisting marginal teachers with professional development plans, many of these suggestions are applicable to building trust in the mentoring process:

- **Acknowledge the challenging work** in which teachers engage
- **Listen**
- Be **slow to judgment**
- **Maintain a consistent** (and above the table) **agenda**
- Acknowledge that the **teaching process is a learning process** and that **mistakes will occur**
- Ensure **confidentiality**
- Set **challenging**, but **attainable goals**
- **Provide supportive resources**

- **Demonstrate sensitivity to and care for the emotional safety of the teacher**

Counsel. Counseling as a facet of mentorship includes providing advice, guidance, and a plan of action. This counsel is a necessary corollary to wisdom as a facet of mentorship. Once you understand the teacher's need in the mentorship process, advice, guidance, and a plan of action is necessary. For example, if a teacher is having difficulty in initiating and maintaining student participation in discussion activities, you might develop with the teacher a plan of action which might include effective questioning and rejoinder behaviors. Perhaps a new teacher is having trouble maintaining student behavior at an acceptable level. You might guide the teacher to a mentor or buddy teacher who excels at, among other things, maintaining student behavior not through intimidation, but through effective instructional practices. Two points are important to consider: (1) The advice and counsel you provide must hinge on your knowledge of the teacher's situation and your knowledge of ways to assist the teacher, and (2) the advice and counsel might also lie in someone other than yourself, such as another staff member, a professional development workshop, or the like. Finally, counsel must include *encouragement*. All of us have mentors; there is nothing like a pep talk or word of encouragement from a trusted mentor to give us a "boost" to keep us going.

Teaching. The overwhelming majority of principals in our schools are former teachers (as it should be). As we noted earlier, our definition of teaching includes providing knowledge and enhancing learning by experience. To be sure, the principal is not the repository of all that is worth knowing about teaching and learning, although we have noted the fundamental knowledge and understanding that principals should possess. Teaching as causing to learn by experience is probably more applicable to the principal's role as a mentor. Ideally, every principal should be able to model effective teaching behaviors; in fact, this is one strategy that a principal can utilize in assisting teachers. However, teaching as causing to learn by experience suggests much more. Principals fulfilling this teaching role should:

- **Be aware of individual professional development opportunities** available to teachers based on teacher needs. Tie professional development to organizational and individual goals and budgetary needs.

- **Utilize** other teachers in the building as **mentor or buddy teachers** (see Frase, 1992, for an excellent discussion of developing a mentor teacher program). Where possible, compensate mentor teachers.
- Empower teachers to examine their teaching as **reflective practitioners** (Sergiovanni, 1991).

In sum, the role of the principal as coach and guide has been conceptualized and presented as formulating expectations and goals and providing the guidance and mentorship necessary for teachers to attain goals. To complete this puzzle, we will next embark on a discussion of the element necessary to gauge whether goals have been attained: The element of feedback.

PROVIDING FEEDBACK

As we have repeatedly noted, feedback is the core job characteristic which influences the degree to which individuals are knowledgeable about the results of their work. Moreover, as a core job characteristic, the feedback designed into a teacher's job is subject to direct influence by the principal.

Everyone wants and has a need to know how they are doing. Feedback provides us with a way of knowing whether we are living up to expectations, if we are attaining goals, and how we can improve our performance. Whether feedback is provided by a supervisor, colleague, student, parent, or community member, or by the activities of the work itself, feedback is an ever present reality for educators. How (not whether) principals structure work to provide feedback and how principals personally provide feedback to teachers is an important part of the mentorship equation and can result in either favorable or unfavorable conditions for teacher motivation (Thomson, 1993).

This discussion of feedback will focus on the principal's role in structuring work activities to provide feedback and personally providing feedback to teachers. To be sure, principals also need to actively seek and be sensitive to feedback about their job performance and the performance of the school as an organization (see the volume in *The School Leadership Library* on "Information Collection"). However, this topic is beyond the scope of our subsequent discussion.

PROVIDING FEEDBACK PERSONALLY

Part of every principal's job is to personally provide feedback to individual teachers and to the teaching staff as a whole. In many cases and depending on the nature of the feedback, providing feedback is one of the most pleasurable aspects of the job; in some cases, it is the least pleasurable part of the job. Yet, teachers seek feedback and are more interested in negative or corrective feedback than none at all (in fact, if you subscribe to a Theory Y view of people, corrective feedback is necessary because of individuals' desire to improve their performance).

Feedback Considerations. There have been volumes written on feedback and how individuals can not only develop feedback skills but also provide effective feedback. These guidelines for developing feedback skills and providing individual feedback come from Hoy and Miskel (1996) and Schmuck and Runkel (1994). Several are illustrated by examples.

- The **intent of feedback must be to assist the teacher**. This caveat is important to remember whether the nature of the feedback is positive or corrective. Which is more damaging to a teacher: (1) Providing positive feedback when corrective feedback is necessary, or (2) providing corrective feedback in a manner which is personally demeaning or does not focus on the behavior that you wish to correct? I would submit that both are equally damaging.
- **Feedback should be non-threatening and be targeted to changeable behavior**. For example, this feedback statement, "I noticed in my last informal observation of your class that students were not afforded adequate wait time to respond to questions," is targeted to readily changeable behavior and is not personally threatening. In contrast, a feedback statement such as "I find your habit of tugging on your ear during class discussions to be distracting," is probably personally threatening and not readily subject to change.

- **Feedback should be specific rather than general**. For example, a statement such as "student behavior in your classroom is not up to par," is far too general. In contrast, a statement such as "I thought the manner in which you rephrased your higher level questions was effective," is more specific and focuses on the teacher's behavior.
- **Feedback should be timely and recent rather than irrelevant and old**. To recognize effective behavior or to correct ineffective behavior, the behavior must be recent enough in the principal's and teacher's mind that both remember the behavior and the context in which the behavior occurred. For one thing, timely corrective feedback minimizes the possibility of the ineffective behavior occurring again. Conversely, timely positive feedback serves two purposes: (1) it lets the teacher know that you notice, and (2) it provides the teacher with recognition of a job well done. Moreover, irrelevant and old feedback can be viewed as a "gotcha" technique. Specifically, " 'Gunnysacks' full of grievances are hard to carry and can burst at inopportune times.' " (Schmuck & Runkel, 1994, p. 135).
- **Feedback should take into account the feelings of the teacher**. This caveat clearly is more applicable to providing corrective feedback than positive feedback. The most useful advice I could offer in this regard is to think about the times you were the recipient of corrective feedback. How did you feel? How did the sender of the feedback handle the situation? If the sender handled the situation effectively, how so? If handled ineffectively, how can you avoid the same pitfalls? (See the accompanying volume of *The School Leadership Library* titled "Oral Expression.") Always preserve the recipient's dignity.

Feedback strategies. Whether we like it or not, the most pervasive feedback mechanism is the formal classroom evaluation that teachers undergo periodically and that seems to be equally distasteful for the evaluator and the teacher. However, this type of formal strategy is only one of a variety of feedback strategies available to the principal. Consider other types of strategies such as:

- **Utilizing satisfaction surveys**. An excellent example of a reliable and valid measure is the *Comprehensive Assessment of School Environments-Information Management System (CASE-IMS)* (Howard & Keefe, 1991) developed by the National Association of Secondary School Principals. This battery consists of school climate, teacher satisfaction, student satisfaction, and parent satisfaction surveys, comes with a friendly user's manual, and provides an excellent means of gauging satisfaction in a manner that protects teacher confidentiality.
- **Informally observing teachers in the classroom**. Better than a periodic formal evaluation, this type of observation better enables principals to observe teachers when less is at stake. Thus, the threat of "supervision" is removed and the principal and teacher can focus on instructional improvement.
- **Conducting informal principal's forums**. One means to accomplish this is to meet informally with grade level teams, academic departments, and even your administrative and counseling teams. In this manner, an informal exchange can take place between the principal and small groups of staff. This exchange provides an excellent vehicle for the principal to provide *and* receive feedback.
- **Providing opportunities for staff to receive feedback on their job performance outside of the school context.** By sending teachers to assessment centers, graduate seminars, or workshops where their performance can be evaluated outside the context of the school, the principal can enhance instructional improvement without teachers feeling threatened by being subjected to evaluative procedures in their own building. Plus, these opportunities give teachers the chance to talk to their colleagues outside the building.

STRUCTURING THE WORK ITSELF TO PROVIDE FEEDBACK

Of course, the degree to which the job itself provides knowledge of work results is central to creating job conditions which enhance teacher motivation. At the same time, it may be the most difficult feedback consideration for the principal and the teacher. At a minimum, structuring the work itself to provide feedback entails two complementary concepts: (1) Enabling teachers to become more effective feedback seekers and sensors (something we could all use), and (2) designing the work itself to provide feedback.

Feedback seeking and sensing. Ashford (1986) suggests that individuals develop two separate feedback seeking strategies to enhance their effectiveness. These strategies are basic and helpful starting points for principals to consider in enabling teachers to become effective feedback seekers and sensors:

- **Scanning and monitoring the environment** for verbal and nonverbal cues. We all do this (perhaps not as effectively as we should). Whether conducting a faculty meeting (gauging the extent to which faculty members are paying attention by determining how many are sleeping!), or conversing with another person, we pay attention to body language, facial expressions, verbal responses, etc., to gain feedback as to how our messages are received. Reminding and encouraging teachers to think about how they sense these cues enables them to be more effective feedback seekers and sensors.
- **Direct inquiry** into how others view and evaluate your behavior. When in doubt, ask!. Even if you are not in doubt, it probably doesn't hurt to ask anyway. One caveat: if you directly inquire, be prepared for the range of answers you might receive. Encourage your teachers to inquire.

Work design. It is also important to design into the work itself means for teachers to receive feedback about their job performance. In addition to enabling teachers to become more effective feedback seekers and sensors, there are other strategies to consider in work design:

- **Informal classroom observations** provide a means for teachers to receive feedback about their job performance. Perhaps a more effective means for conducting informal classroom observations is to build into the work itself opportunities for **team teaching and peer observation**.
- Enabling and assisting teachers to become **reflective practitioners** about their own teaching. ". . .[I]nformed by theoretical knowledge on the one hand and by interacting with the context of practice on the other" (Sergiovanni, 1991, p. 7), reflective practitioners are able to more readily discern the effectiveness of their actions by observing the context in which their actions occur and constructing feedback from the context. Among others, the principal can enable and assist teachers to become reflective practitioners by *providing time for teachers to discuss teaching episodes* with colleagues and/or the principal and to think about their own teaching practices and their effects on students, by *selecting supervision options* which best suit individual teacher needs, and by simply *encouraging staff to think and reflect* on their own practices.

SUMMARY

In this chapter we examined the principal's role in providing mentorship to teachers. We began by defining what a mentor is, what personal characteristics an effective mentor should possess, and the different roles a principal plays as mentor. We operationally defined mentorship as the principal's role in providing coaching and guidance and in providing individual and collective feedback to the teaching staff. Effectiveness at coaching and guidance is necessary to enhance the probability that a given work effort will result in a desired level of performance (*expectancy*), while effectiveness at providing feedback is necessary for teachers to gain knowledge of the results of their work; both are necessary to create conditions for teacher motivation.

We then noted the principal's role in coaching and guidance. This role includes setting expectations and goals as well as providing the guidance (or mentorship) necessary to attain expectations and goals. Finally, we noted the role of the principal in providing feedback to teaching staff by discussing ideas for the principal to consider in providing feedback, by considering strategies that the principal can use to provide feedback (individually and collectively as well as formally and informally), and by noting ways that the principal can structure feedback as part of teachers' work itself.

Mentorship is important. Each of us has a mentor and has been a mentor to others. It is not realistic to assume that the principal is or can be the mentor for every teacher in the building. In fact, the principal's ultimate success as a mentor probably lies in his or her ability to create opportunities for teachers in the building to serve as mentors for their colleagues. Even so, it is critical for the principal as building leader to possess the characteristics of a mentor for three reasons: (1) The principal will mentor (in the true sense of the word) others in the building, (2) by virtue of the principal's position power, teachers will seek advice and feedback from the principal, and (3) the principal's role as a mentor can create conditions for teacher motivation.

ACTION PLAN

- Assess yourself against the four characteristics of mentorship offered at the beginning of the chapter. In which characteristics are you strong; in which characteristics are you less than strong?
- Examine the expectations you place on your staff collectively, and yourself individually. Are they clear, difficult, attainable, and continually articulated? Do your teachers clearly understand your expectations of them? If not, might this ambiguity be stifling staff motivation?
- Examine goals which have been set for the organization, yourself, and individual teachers. Have teachers bought into the goals? Have they been involved in setting goals, especially personal professional goals? Are goals prioritized? Are they capable of being evaluated?
- Consider implementing individual work plans for your administrative and teaching staff. While work plans

tend to be difficult and time consuming at first, they have the effect of putting down on paper staff members' goals and gaining greater commitment to attaining the goals.

- Examine your role as guide. Perhaps even assess your teachers' perceptions of you as a guide or mentor against the four criteria we have discussed earlier. In particular, do your teachers view you as knowledgeable and trustworthy?
- Assess your effectiveness in providing feedback against the criteria we discussed in this chapter. Is feedback designed to benefit teachers, aimed at specific and changeable behavior, and timely? Do your words and actions show consideration for teachers' feelings, especially when feedback is corrective?
- Assess your feedback systems. Think beyond the formal evaluation system as a means for providing feedback. Add at least one informal feedback mechanism that reaches all teaching staff.
- Begin to improve your ability and the ability of the staff to seek and sense feedback from the environment. Start with listening and observation skills.
- Consider ways to design teachers work activities to incorporate additional feedback, e.g., peer observation and reflective practice.
- Are feedback systems based on student performance?

SUGGESTED READINGS

Hoy, W.K., & Miskel, C.G. (1996). *Educational administration: Theory, research, practice* (5th ed.). New York: McGraw-Hill. (See especially Chapter 4, titled "Individuals in Schools", and Chapter 11, titled "Communicating".)

Schmuck, R.A, & Runkel, P.J. (1994). *The handbook of organizational development in schools and colleges* (2nd ed.). Prospect Heights, IL: Waveland Press, Inc. (See especially Chapter 4, titled "Clarifying Communication".)

Sergiovanni, T.J. (1991). *The principalship: A reflective practice perspective* (2nd ed.). Boston: Allyn & Bacon. (See especially Chapter 1, titled "The Nature of Reflective Practice in the Principalship.")

Yukl, G.A. (1989). *Leadership in organizations* (2nd ed.). Englewood Cliffs, NJ: Prentice-Hall. (See especially Chapter 7, titled "An Integrative Model of Effective Managerial Behavior.")

6

Rewarding and Recognizing Effective Performance

" . . .although what gets rewarded often gets done, the reverse is likely to be true: what does not get rewarded does not get done. In other words, the rule focuses one's attention and narrows one's response to work. Further, for the rule to be sustained, a busy kind of leadership is required. Leaders must constantly monitor the exchange of rewards for work, guess which rewards are of interest to workers and which are not, and figure out ways to keep this exchange going. As a result, workers become increasingly dependent on rewards and on their leaders to motivate them. 'What gets rewarded gets done' discourages people from becoming self-managed and self-motivated." (Sergiovanni, 1992, pp. 24-25)

Our discussion thus far has centered on how principals can create conditions for teachers to become self-managed and self-motivated. What a shame it would be if the ideas we have discussed to create these conditions were to be negated by strict adherence to the "what is rewarded gets done" rule of motivation discussed at length in Chapter 1.

At the same time, rewarding and recognizing are important means for leaders and organizations to clarify performance expectations, enhance job satisfaction, and motivate individuals within the organization (Hoy & Miskel, 1996; Yukl, 1989). Properly conceived and implemented, rewarding and recognizing effective performance is a tool in the principal's repertoire to create conditions for teacher motivation; improperly conceived and implemented, rewarding and recognizing is not a means of motivating, but rather a means of gaining compliance (Kohn, in Brandt, 1995). Therefore, this chapter will be devoted to the general subject of rewarding and recognizing effective teacher performance. After examining perspectives on rewarding and recognizing, our discussion will include issues to consider in rewarding and recognizing effective teacher performance. Finally, we will examine actual reward and recognition strategies that principals can utilize to create conditions for teacher motivation.

PERSPECTIVES

In this section, three themes will be addressed. ***First,*** I will define, compare, and contrast the concepts of rewards and incentives. ***Second,*** I will use two theoretical perspectives to highlight the importance of rewarding and recognizing effective performance. ***Third,*** I will summarize three reward typologies that can inform the principal's role in rewarding and recognizing effective performance.

REWARDS AND INCENTIVES

Probably the place to begin this discussion is with the concept of incentive. Incentives are inducements or rewards received by individuals from the organization in exchange for productivity (Hoy & Miskel, 1996). Although often used interchangeably, there is a slight difference in the concepts of reward and incentive. An incentive is a reward, but is more specific than a reward because of the inducement factor. Specifically, "rewards only become incentives when they are contemplated in advance and have the capacity to change work behavior" (Hoy & Miskel, 1991, p. 190). Under this distinction, a principal might provide a *reward* to all teachers (perhaps an hour lunch on an inservice day) where *no behavior change* was necessary to receive the reward. Conversely, a principal might provide an *incentive* to individual teachers (perhaps an early release if all grades are turned in early at the end of a grading period) which is obviously *contingent on teachers' behavior*. In our discussion, the term reward will be used to also refer to incentives; distinctions on the basis of inducement will be made as necessary. In addition, the terms reward and incentive can also be thought of as valued work outcomes; in fact, I tend to prefer this connotation because it seems to avoid conflict with the "what gets rewarded gets done" rule of motivation.

THEORETICAL PERSPECTIVES ON THE IMPORTANCE OF REWARDS AND RECOGNITION

Needs Hierarchy and Two-Factor Theories. Two theoretical perspectives noted in Chapter 1 consider the importance of rewards and recognition in creating conditions for teacher motivation. In Figure 1.3 we compared the Porter's (1961) revised Needs Hierarchy Theory with Herzberg's (Herzberg et al., 1959) Two-Factor Theory. When considering rewards as valued work outcomes, we note that the descriptors of each level of the needs hierarchy and the descriptors of the hygiene and motivation factors are nothing more than realized or potential outcomes of being in an organization. What we further notice is that when we ascend both the needs hierarchy and the vertical axis describing the Two-Factor Theory, the less "tangible" and less "extrinsic" these outcomes become. Moreover, when we consider that motivation is that inner state which prompts us to behave in certain ways to satisfy important needs, we can argue that the lower level needs and the hygiene factors require less prompting to behave in certain ways to satisfy these needs than do the higher level needs. For example, once we were accepted into a teaching position, security level needs and hygiene factors as such salary, health and retirement benefits, and working conditions were as much the same for us as those similarly situated to us. In contrast, to fulfill higher level needs such as recognition, achievement, and autonomy, requires of us greater motivation to behave in certain ways (assuming that fulfilling these needs are important to us). Therefore, the extent to which these quite similar theoretical perspectives suggest that less extrinsic and intangible outcomes (i.e., higher level needs) tend to enhance conditions for teacher motivation, to a similar extent these perspectives also suggest that opportunities to fulfill these needs should be considered by principals in rewarding and recognizing effective performance.

Expectancy Model of Motivation. The second theoretical perspective which also considers the importance of rewards and outcomes in the "motivation equation" is the Expectancy Model of Motivation depicted in Figure 1.4. We have thus far focused on the *expectancy* probability as it informs us of how principals can create conditions to increase the likelihood that teachers' efforts will result in a desired performance level (see especially Chapters 4 and 5). The other probability in this model which influences individual motivation is *instrumentality*, or the probability that a desired performance will result in a valued and desired outcome. For example, if a building principal and his or her staff realize that a monetary reward is forthcoming from the state if a certain percentage of students pass a state mandated, criterion referenced exam, and the principal and the staff value this reward, then this enhanced instrumentality probability acts as a motivating force to attain this percentage of students passing.

An individual example might better illustrate instrumentality. Suppose a teacher wishes to become part of a multi-disciplinary team which teaches middle school at-risk students in a "school-within-a-school" format. The principal may believe that the teacher is not quite ready for this assignment, but suggests a graduate seminar or other professional development opportunity to enhance this teacher's readiness to be part of the team. If the teacher feels that his or her performance will be enhanced by professional development (*expectancy*), he or she will be motivated to seek additional training. Moreover (and most pertinent to this discussion), if the teacher believes that his or her enhanced performance will result in being assigned to the team (*instrumentality*), he or she will be motivated to seek the training. Based on this second example, one can think of two strategies by which the principal can enhance the instrumentality probability. ***First***, the principal can structure the work itself to provide opportunities for individuals to satisfy this need. ***Second***, the principal can monitor and provide desired and the valued work outcome for the teacher (this applies to groups of teachers as well) based on this teacher's effective performance. In this example, the principal used both strategies. While both categories of strategies are important for the principal to consider, our theoretical perspective's suggest that more of the first strategy and less of the second strategy is more desirable for creating conditions of motivation through rewarding and recognizing effective performance.

REWARD TYPOLOGIES

At least three typologies or classifications of rewards are found in the organizational leadership literature. While the categories of rewards in each typology are not mutually exclusive, these typologies provide a good way to think about different types of rewards that are available to teachers. Each typology and examples of rewards in each classification are discussed in the following paragraphs. Figure 6.1 summarizes these typologies and their relationships to one another.

Specific and general rewards. First classified by Chester Barnard (1938), these types of rewards are distinguished by their definition, orientation, and by the leader's ability to influence their distribution. *Specific* rewards are well-defined, oriented to individuals, and their distribution is more subject to the leader's control. Examples of specific rewards (Hoy & Miskel, 1991) include material rewards, such as salary, benefits, and opportunities and support for travel; nonmaterial rewards, such as prestige, recognition, and advancement; pleasant physical working conditions; and the opportunity to work in an organization congruent with one's own values, ideals, and goals.

General rewards, in contrast, are less-well defined (since they tend to be nonmaterial), oriented to groups of individuals in the organization, and thus tend to be less under administrative influence in their distribution. Examples of general rewards (Hoy & Miskel, 1991) include social compatibility, opportunities to work in a somewhat stable environment, greater participation opportunities, and informal organization (interpersonal) support for proper attitudes. Again, because these rewards are nonmaterial and somewhat ill-defined, their distribution is less subject to administrative influence.

The distinction between specific and general rewards is important for three reasons. ***First***, both categories of rewards encompass many of the motivation and hygiene factors identified by Herzberg (see Fig. 1.2) to contribute to employee satis-

FIGURE 6.1. RELATIONSHIP OF REWARD TYPOLOGIES

Reward Typology	Extrinsic	Ancillary	Intrinsic (psychic)
General	Peer acceptance Collegial interaction Interpersonal support Working in stable environment Participation Social compatibility		Achievement Personal & professional growth Work itself Autonomy Feelings of influence Efficacy Reaching students
Specific	Material rewards salary benefits travel opportunities/ support Working conditions Nonmaterial rewards prestige recognition advancement Working in organization congruent with values and goals Promotion Teaching assignments	Working conditions Job security Stability of schedule	

faction and dissatisfaction. Specific rewards which align with Herzberg's hygiene factors include material rewards and working conditions. General rewards which align with the hygienes include social compatibility, informal organization support, and the opportunity to work in a stable environment. Specific rewards which align with the motivation factors include nonmaterial rewards and the opportunity to work in an organization congruent with personal goals, values, and ideals. General rewards which tend to align with the motivation factors include increased participation opportunities. ***Second,*** and by application, both specific and general rewards are either present or absent in teachers' work; thus, the presence and absence of these rewards can contribute to either the dissatisfaction and satisfaction of teachers. Therefore, any system of rewards or incentives should take both specific and general rewards into account. ***Third,*** the rewards which tend to contribute to the satisfaction of teachers tend to be nonmaterial and less tangible.

Extrinsic and intrinsic rewards. As defined by Hoy & Miskel (1996), extrinsic rewards are provided by others (i.e., the organization or individuals), while intrinsic rewards are provided by the individual to him or herself. *Extrinsic* rewards tend to be tangible and include money, recognition, promotion, reduced class sizes, desirable teaching assignments, collegial interaction, influence in the school, etc. *Intrinsic* rewards tend to intangible and affective and include feelings of achievement, responsibility, efficacy, and personal and professional growth. As intrinsic rewards are self-granted, they are clearly under the individual's control, while extrinsic rewards are more susceptible to external control.

Much like the distinction between specific and general rewards, the distinction between extrinsic and intrinsic rewards are similar to the distinction between the hygiene and motivators found by Herzberg et al. (1959). While the motivation factors of advancement, recognition, and responsibility tend to be extrinsic in nature, the factors of achievement, the work itself, and professional and personal growth are clearly intrinsic in nature. However, even though the literature highlights the importance of teacher intrinsic motivation, school leaders should not dismiss the importance of extrinsic rewards (Hoy & Miskel, 1996), particularly in providing opportunities for recognition, advancement, and responsibility. At the very least, sufficient presence of tangible extrinsic rewards minimizes the probability that teachers will experience dissatisfaction. At the very most, the presence of certain extrinsic rewards and intrinsic rewards can contribute to the probability that teachers will experience satisfaction.

Lortie's typology. This typology was offered by Dan C. Lortie (1975) in his famous *Schoolteacher: A Sociological Study.* Lortie classified rewards into three categories: Extrinsic, ancillary, and psychic. *Extrinsic* rewards exist regardless of who fills a teaching role, are experienced (to a greater or lesser degree) by all role incumbents, are objective, and include the "'earnings'" (p. 101) of money, prestige, and power. According to Lortie, teachers are relatively unable to exercise influence over extrinsic rewards and, with limited exceptions, have limited opportunities to increase these rewards over the long term.

Ancillary rewards tend to be available to all teachers, are objective or specific in nature, but also have a subjective quality. For example, in a school district teachers might often be asked to serve on a district level committee. This ancillary aspect of teaching is objective in nature. However, the subjective value of this ancillary benefit might differ between teachers. While one teacher might view being chosen for a committee to be an opportunity for professional growth, another teacher might view being chosen as an intrusion on valuable time. Thus, ancillary rewards are objective work outcomes which may be viewed either positively or negatively. Other examples of ancillary rewards noted by Lortie include working conditions, job security, and stability of schedule.

Finally, *psychic* or intrinsic rewards are completely subjective and are granted by teachers to themselves during the course of work activities. Because of this subjectivity, these rewards differ within each teacher and are much harder to identify. The prime example of a psychic reward identified by Lortie was the knowledge that a teacher had "reached" a student and that the student had learned. Other examples of psychic rewards included opportunities to become more effective professionally (reading and planning for classes, development of classroom management skills), to associate with young people, and to associate with colleagues. In his study, Lortie found that teachers identified psychic rewards as the major source of work satisfaction.

Summary. While these three typologies (again, see Fig. 6.1 for their relationships) are not prescriptive in nature, they do provide different ways to classify and think about rewards and incentives. Moreover, all three are important for principals to consider in rewarding and recognizing effective teacher performance.

Five generalizations can be drawn from these typologies. ***First***, the profession of teaching is not one which will make teachers (or administrators!) independently wealthy. Indeed, the focus of reward systems has been on and continues to be on intrinsic rewards which can be derived from the work itself and granted by individuals to themselves (Hoy & Miskel, 1996). ***Second,*** even though this focus has been on intrinsic rewards, principals are ill-advised to ignore extrinsic rewards, particularly those of recognition, responsibility, and advancement, in the motivation equation. ***Third,*** both specific and general rewards, even though they differ by definition, orientation (individual vs. organization), and susceptibility to influence by administrators, are important for principals to consider in rewarding and recognizing effective performance because examples of each type of reward can contribute to teacher dissatisfaction or satisfaction. ***Fourth,*** intrinsic or psychic rewards seem to contribute to the motivation of teachers more so than extrinsic or ancillary rewards. ***Finally,*** although teachers grant intrinsic rewards to themselves, the principal can create conditions whereby these intrinsic rewards are more likely to be granted.

ISSUES TO CONSIDER IN REWARDING AND RECOGNIZING

With these perspectives in mind, we can now consider several issues or guidelines for principals to consider in rewarding and recognizing effective teacher performance (Again, part of the principal's strategy should be to build into the work itself opportunities for many of the job characteristics we have discussed in preceding chapters, i.e., participation, teamwork, collegiality, intellectual stimulation, challenge, autonomy, innovation, feedback, etc.). These issues or guidelines are culled from much reading and personal experience; in particular, see the following sources (Bartell, 1987; Blase & Blase, 1994; Blase & Kirby, 1992; Cresap, McCormick & Paget, 1984; Frase, 1992; Thomson, 1993; and Yukl, 1989).

- **Relate rewards and recognition to work-related performance.**
- **Use rewards and recognition to empower teachers, and not to control or gain their compliance.**

- **Analyze the intent of your rewarding and recognizing behaviors**. Bartell (1987) asserts that there are four intents to consider in rewarding and recognizing teacher performance: (1) Attracting teachers, (2) retaining teachers, (3) improving teachers' performance, and (4) enhancing teachers' professional status. These intents provide one way of looking at purposes of recognizing and rewarding.
- **Be aware of teachers' valued rewards and work outcomes** (Thomson, 1993). Although this is an important consideration, my only caution is that you, as principal, ***do not become the reward for work "exchange monitor."*** In general, you probably have a pretty good idea of what your staff values; this awareness can inform you of rewards or incentives that might empower your teachers to greater performance.
- **Be aware of your teachers' work activities**. In other words, if you do not already know, find out about what is going on in your teachers' professional lives. You might find that one of your teachers has been recognized by his or her university as an outstanding student, has been appointed to a statewide committee, or has done something in his or her classroom to motivate students. These are important opportunities for rewarding and recognizing your teaching staff. Therefore, be visible and available, particularly at times of the day when teachers have time to talk (lunch and before or after the school day).
- **When using enrichment activities as a reward or recognition for effective performance** (e.g., rewarding an effective teacher by providing an opportunity for the teacher to conduct a staff development workshop), provide the support necessary for the teacher to conduct the activity. Support might include a monetary stipend, public recognition, released time to prepare for the workshop, and so on. In addition, do not overload your most effective teachers with too many additional responsibilities.

- When recognizing and praising a teacher, whether publicly or privately, **be sincere** and relate the praise and recognition to the teacher's professional work activities. Do not "blow smoke"; teachers will pick up on this immediately.
- **Schedule time and opportunities** for teacher rewards and recognition. Think about using the public address system (judiciously, of course), a daily bulletin, notes in teachers' boxes, formal activities designed for teachers (dinners, student recognition activities, etc.), and news releases to the local media.
- Reward and recognize teacher performance that is **determined by teachers' skills** rather than luck and **that can be observed** (Yukl, 1989).
- **Find ways to provide the entire faculty and staff** with tokens of your appreciation for their work. Consider business cards, school emblazoned coffee mugs, or other tangible tokens that let the entire staff know you appreciate them. These are not even rewards or incentives; they are really expressions of appreciation.

REWARDING AND RECOGNIZING STRATEGIES

In the previous section, I referred to the work of Carol Bartell (1987) who suggested four purposes for providing incentives to teachers: (1) Attracting teachers, (2) retaining teachers, (3) improving teacher performance, and (4) enhancing teacher status. Bartell used these four intents and five different categories of incentives (monetary compensation, career status, awards and recognition, professional responsibility, and workplace conditions), to develop an Incentive Matrix (see Fig. 6.2). To be sure, this matrix does not prescribe a "one best way" to reward and recognize. However, it gives principals a way to think about how to reward and recognize effective teacher performance by classifying objectives and types of incentives.

Bartell does not actually plug specific rewards into cells of the matrix; rather, she provides specific examples of each category of incentive. As the building, the principal should consider and decide (preferably collaboratively) which specific incentive should be provided based on the category of incentive, and the objective to be served. She does however, suggest several specific incentives for each category; these incentives and other examples are provided below. Please keep in mind that specific incentives in these categories tend to overlap.

Monetary compensation. Bartell suggests several incentives under monetary compensation. Many of these incentives are probably better suited for the objectives of attracting and retaining teachers. Indeed, providing monetary compensation tends to be centered in the district office rather than in the building. Yet, there are a many things that principals can provide or lobby the district to provide:

- Money to attend conferences, conduct workshops, and purchase materials
- Salary stipends for teacher leaders, i.e., department chairs and team leaders
- Providing tuition reimbursement to take graduate classes
- Providing money for teacher membership in one professional association
- Paid sabbaticals
- Securing summer employment
- Merit or performance based pay

Career status incentives. These incentives include:

- Part-time teaching
- Team teaching
- Job sharing
- Position exchanges within the building, district, or between districts
- Career ladder plans
- Administrative & supervisory internships
- Sabbaticals
- Working on team projects and task forces

Awards and recognition. These rewards or outcomes include:

- Letters of recognition from you, the superintendent, or the board

FIGURE 6.2. INCENTIVE MATRIX

Copyright 1987 North Central Regional Educational Laboratory. Reprinted with permission from Bartell, C. (1987). *Incentives that enhance the teaching profession: Background paper*. Elmhurst, IL: North Central Regional Labaratory.

Incentive	Attract	Retain	Improve Performance	Enhance Status
Monetary Compensation				
Career Status				
Awards & Recognition				
Professional Responsibility				
Workplace Conditions				

- Recognition in building or district newsletters or in the print or broadcast media
- Special ceremonies to honor outstanding teachers
- Personal private and public verbal recognition
- Designating a "Teacher of the (week, month, and/or year)" and procuring business or foundation stipends for the winners
- Providing opportunities for current and former students to recognize teachers
- Awarding honorary degrees to teachers
- Instituting reward programs (see Frase, 1992, for guidelines for building and implementing a teacher reward program in your building)
- Providing opportunities for teachers to become more visible in the community (e.g., recommending teachers to speak at Rotary, Lions, and other community groups, encourage service to the community, etc.)

Professional responsibility. These rewards or valued outcomes include:

- Serving as a mentor or master teacher
- Supervision of student teachers
- Released time for curriculum development
- Serving as a peer coach or mentor
- Chairing or participating on special committees
- Participation in decision-making (see Chapter Two)
- Participating in and leading staff development activities
- Providing job exchanges with business and industry
- Providing summer employment opportunities (curriculum development, summer school administrative positions, teaching either at school or perhaps in a community college, etc.)

Workplace condition incentives. These incentives and outcomes include the following:

- Adequate preparation and planning time
- Paraprofessional support
- Opportunities to observe and be observed by peers

- Teacher input into such activities as textbook selection, curriculum development and revision, course design, student placement, codes of conduct, attendance policies, personnel policies, long range planning, and course scheduling
- On site child care
- Staff wellness programs
- Adequate work space and pleasant working conditions

There is no question that not all types of incentives or valued outcomes have been covered. Hopefully, these incentives, along with an objective for providing them, will provide you with additional and better ideas to create conditions for teacher motivation through rewarding and recognizing effective performance.

SUMMARY

In this chapter we examined the role of the principal in creating conditions for teacher motivation through rewarding and recognizing effective performance. We began our discussion by noting an important caveat: while rewarding and recognizing effective performance are important in creating these conditions, it must be done without adherence to the "what gets rewarded gets done" rule of motivation. Moreover, rewarding and recognizing effective performance must be done with the intent to empower, not to gain control or compliance.

Although the terms reward and incentives were used interchangeably, we noted distinctions between the terms. The basic difference between the two is that incentives infer that a change in behavior is necessary to attain an incentive, while no change might be necessary to receive a reward. This distinction in mind, I submitted that "valued work outcomes" might be the best alternative for reward and incentive.

We then noted theoretical perspectives on the importance of rewards and recognition and three reward typologies. With regard to theoretical perspectives, we noted the overlay of Porter's revised Needs Hierarchy Theory and Herzberg's Motivator-Hygiene Theory. In this examination, we found that as we moved up the hierarchy of needs, the valued outcomes tended to move from extrinsic and tangible to intrinsic and less tangible. We also noted the Expectancy Theory of Motivation, which suggested that motivation is influenced by instrumentality, or the probability that a desired performance level would lead to a valued work outcome.

The three typologies of rewards or valued work outcomes we examined were: specific-general (Barnard, 1938), extrinsic-intrinsic (Hoy & Miskel, 1996), and extrinsic-ancillary-psychic (Lortie, 1975). Specific rewards, exemplified by material rewards, nonmaterial rewards, physical working conditions, and working in an organization with values congruent to one's own, are well defined, individually oriented, and more readily subject to administrative control. General rewards, exemplified by social compatibility, working in a routinized environment, greater participation opportunities, and informal organization support, are less well defined, group oriented, and less subject to administrative influence. We also posited that both specific and general rewards or valued work outcomes are important in rewarding and recognizing effective performance.

The extrinsic-intrinsic and extrinsic-ancillary-psychic typologies are quite similar, with the major difference being that ancillary work outcomes, while objective in nature, are viewed subjectively by different persons. Extrinsic rewards are granted by others (individual or organizational), while intrinsic rewards are self-bestowed. While research evidence cited suggests greater work satisfaction from intrinsic rewards, extrinsic rewards should not be discounted.

This chapter closed with two themes: the first theme centered on issues for the principal to consider in rewarding and recognizing effective performance, and the second theme focused on an incentive strategy that principals can use to more effectively create motivation conditions through this role. Under the second theme, we drew heavily on the incentive matrix of Bartell (1987) to consider how different types of valued work outcomes interact with purposes of incentives to suggest a strategy for principals to use in rewarding and recognizing effective performance. Finally, we listed several examples of valued work outcomes for each category of incentive, careful to note that these are ideas for principals' consideration and not a "one best way" to reward and recognize.

On at least two occasions in this chapter, I have alluded to the importance of rewards and recognition for effective performance. They are not so important, however, to be the only strategy for principals to use to create conditions for motivation. In combination with the topics that we have discussed, rewarding and recognizing should be viewed as one of many strategies available to principals to create these conditions for teacher motivation.

One personal note to which I trust that each of you can relate. Each of us has received professional recognition for work done successfully. Think back to one of those occasions. What did you take from this occasion? If you received a monetary reward, it's already gone. If you received a plaque, it might be in storage. If you received a trip to some exotic location, you've already returned. What you and I take from the occasion is the recognition for a job well done, the feeling of achievement and accomplishment, and the desire to live up to the expectations we have created for ourselves. That's what we take from teaching!

ACTION PLAN

- Examine the rewards and valued work outcomes available to you and your staff in light of the typologies we examined. Are you using what is available and doing so effectively? What types of incentives are available to you that you are not using and could?
- Filter your behaviors in rewarding and recognizing effective performance through the guidelines offered in this chapter. Do you consider these guidelines in rewarding and recognizing? Are there other guidelines pertinent to your unique situation?
- Assess your rewarding strategies in light of the matrix presented in Figure 6.2. Are you considering the multiple purposes of incentives? Are your incentives varied? What other incentives at your disposal or that you can think of would fit into matrix cells?
- Find at least three additional ways to recognize individual teachers and your faculty for their performance. In at least one way, involve students in the recognition.

SUGGESTED READINGS

Blase, J., & Kirby, P.C. (1992). *Bringing out the best in teachers: What effective principals do.* Newbury Park, CA: Corwin Press. (See especially Chapter 2 titled "The Power of Praise.")

Frase, L.E. (1992). *Maximizing people power in schools: Managing and motivating teachers and staff.* Newbury Park, CA: Corwin Press. (See especially Chapter 2 titled "Teacher Burnout and Mediocrity: The Antidote is Professional Development and Motivation" for guidelines in developing a teacher reward program.)

Lortie, D.C. (1975). *Schoolteacher: A sociological study.* Chicago: The University of Chicago Press. (See especially Chapter 4 titled "Career and Work Rewards".)

7

PORTFOLIO OF ONE*

> *"In short, respondents* (teachers) *want an approachable principal who eschews rulemaking and close supervision and is equitable in his* (her) *dealings with faculty members. He* (she) *should be knowledgeable and firm with both parents and students. The qualities teachers mention meet their needs for autonomy* **and** *support; the principal should moderate his* (her) *use of authority over teachers but assert it in relationships with parents, students, and dilatory colleagues. These teachers do not question the rightfulness of the principal's authority, but they seek to appropriate it to their ends."*
>
> (Lortie, 1975, p. 198, emphasis in original, parentheses mine.)

Have teachers' desires, as articulated by Lortie, for the personal characteristics of principals changed much over the last 20 years? My guess is probably not too much. We have noted that principals, in their quest to create conditions for teacher motivation, provide mentorship by holding high and attainable expectations for teacher performance. Based on Lortie's findings and the research of others (Blase & Blase, 1994; Blase & Kirby, 1992; Rosenholtz, 1989), it is probably safe to say that teachers' expectations for principals are on an even higher plane.

Up to this point, we have focused on strategies that principals can use to create conditions for teacher motivation. We have framed much of our discussion around the Job Characteristics Model of Work Motivation (Fig. 1.5), which suggests that an individual's psychological states of experiencing that work is meaningful; of experiencing responsibility for work outcomes,

---

*Blase & Kirby (1992, p. 33).

and of having knowledge of work results, are critical to that person realizing intrinsic motivation in and from work activities. These critical psychological states are in turn influenced by the degree to which the job provides *skill variety, task identity,* and *task significance* (*experienced meaningfulness of the work*); *autonomy* (*experienced responsibility for work outcomes*); and *feedback* (*knowledge of work results*). As we have continually noted, the principal, while not able to directly control the critical psychological states, through the core job characteristics can influence the degree to which teachers can experience these critical psychological states.

One of the variables present in the Job Characteristics Model is the teacher's need for professional and personal growth. This variable, while noted in Chapter 1, probably did not receive the attention it deserved. This variable suggests that teachers with a high need for personal and professional growth will more positively respond to and function in work activities with these core job characteristics present than will teachers with a lower need for personal and professional growth. This moderator is important because it acknowledges the personal dimension in each teacher. The reality of the situation is this: A principal might be most successful in designing teachers' work to provide the five core job characteristics necessary to create conditions for teacher motivation, but if an individual teacher does not have a high need for personal and professional growth, these conditions will not lead to teacher motivation. While I believe that these teachers are in the overwhelming minority, the obligation of the principal in these cases is to move these teachers out of their teaching roles.

This personal dimension, with stronger reason, must also apply to the principal. That is, the principal must have a strong need for personal and professional growth to function effectively to create conditions for teacher motivation. The principal cannot rely on just the power of the position, or on the power to reward and punish, to motivate teachers. At best, these sources of power will gain temporary compliance; at worst, they will alienate the teaching staff and "de" motivate them. In short, then, the principal must possess certain personal characteristics to effectively create conditions for teacher motivation.

I chose the title "Portfolio of One" (Blase and Kirby, 1992, p. 33) to attempt to convey the message that as the person in charge of the school, the principal is the person to whom teachers look for guidance, stability, resources, encouragement, and leadership. Portfolio connotes a collection of materials which represents one's work. In this chapter, portfolio connotes the collection of personal characteristics that principals absolutely must possess or develop to function effectively in creating conditions of teacher motivation.

This chapter consists of three sections. In the first, we will examine a typology of sources of interpersonal power. In the second, we will note a collection of personal characteristics for principals to possess. Finally, we will close with "twenty questions" that principals can ask themselves to assess their portfolio.

SOURCES OF PRINCIPAL INTERPERSONAL POWER

This typology of the sources of interpersonal power was developed by John French and Bertram Raven (1968) and is cited in numerous volumes on organizational behavior and leadership (see, for example, Daft, 1988; Hoy & Miskel, 1996; Yukl, 1989). According to French and Raven, and as applied to schools, principals enjoy (to a greater or lesser extent) five sources of interpersonal power. The first three of these sources flow from the position the principal occupies in the organization, while the final two emanate directly from the principal him or herself. These sources of interpersonal power are:

- **Legitimate power**. The principal's legitimate power directly flows from the position he or she occupies and plays a part in the degree to which the principal can influence teacher behavior. As applied to the teacher/principal relationship, French and Raven (1968) define this power as that which comes from teachers' values which acknowledge that principals have a right to influence teachers and that teachers have an obligation to accept this influence. Obvious examples of this power include the ability of the principal to direct teachers to do certain things like appear at work on time, turn in lesson plans, and follow a special education student's individual education plan. Teachers understand that they are obligated to follow the principal's directives which lie within a specified zone of the principal's responsibility; the strength of the principal's legitimate power is determined by the closeness of the directive to the area of responsibility (Hoy & Miskel, 1996). For example, a principal may direct a teacher to submit a discipline referral when removing a student from class and sending the student to the office. If the teacher elects to send the student, the referral is very likely to accompany the student. Yet, this directive might easily be sidestepped by the teacher tolerating the behavior and not sending the student to the office.

- **Reward power**. As the second of the three sources of power which emanate from the position that the principal occupies, reward power is the principal's ability to influence teachers by rewarding desirable behavior. We have discussed the potpourri of resources available to the principal in Chapter 4; an example of the principal utilizing reward power might be assigning a teacher who has shown considerable instructional improvement to an honors class or a gifted and talented grade level class. Three considerations are important to the principal's reward power: (1) The rewards under the control of the principal must be of value to the teacher, (2) the principal must exercise control over the rewards (Hoy & Miskel, 1996), and (3) the teacher must perceive that the principal exercises control over rewards. In our current example, if a department or grade level chair has the authority to allocate teaching assignments with cursory approval by the principal, the principal's control over this reward would be minimized and might not be a viable reward power option.
- **Coercive power**. Coercive power, or the ability of the principal to punish undesirable teacher behavior, is the third source of power flowing from the principal's position. For example, a principal might place a letter of reprimand in a teacher's personnel file for repeated failure to carry out assigned duties, or might even recommend a teacher's termination or perhaps a transfer to a less desirable campus in the district. The influence of

the principal's coercive power hinges on the probability of the teacher receiving a punishment for undesirable behavior, coupled with the severity of the punishment (Hoy & Miskel, 1996).

Of course, one might suspect that coercive power is the least effective interpersonal power source. Yukl (1989) even goes as far to say that repeated use of coercive power by the leader can result in "coercive counterpower" (p. 19) exercised by subordinates; examples of coercive counterpower include sabotaging performance evaluations, filing grievances or lawsuits, demonstrating, going over the leader's head, and striking.

- **Expert power**. This source of power is one of two sources which flow directly from the principal. Expert power is the ability of the principal to influence teacher behavior based on his or her special skills and knowledge which might be useful for in solving problems or carrying out important tasks. For example, an elementary principal with special knowledge of a particular student's background might share this knowledge with the child's teacher in a way that will improve the teacher's effectiveness in "reaching" the child. Or, any principal with knowledge of recent court holdings in special education law might use this knowledge to influence the behavior of both regular and special education teachers. In these examples, teachers are influenced to behave in certain ways based on the knowledge they need and that the principal possesses. These examples underscore three important points (Hoy & Miskel, 1996; Yukl, 1989). Specifically, the ability of the principal to influence teachers through expert power depends on: (1) The extent to which teachers are in need of the principal's skills and knowledge, (2) the importance of the task or problem for which teachers need assistance, and (3) teachers' perceptions of the principal's relevant knowledge and skills. While principals cannot be experts in all phases of the school operation, it is an important implication that principals "keep current" on issues of importance to the staff.

- **Referent power**. The second source of power not dependent on the principal's position in the school, referent power connotes the ability of the principal to influence teachers' behavior based on teachers' identification with, liking of, and loyalty to the principal. For example, a teacher who might not otherwise follow a principal's suggestion to attend a professional development seminar on assertive discipline might do so based on his or her loyalty toward and personal admiration of the principal. Yukl (1989, p. 24) states it best:

  The referent power of a leader over subordinates depends upon feelings of friendship and loyalty developed slowly over a long period of time. The referent power of a leader is increased by the leader's *acting friendly* and *considerate, showing concern* for the needs and feelings of others, *demonstrating trust and respect*, and *treating people fairly*. Referent power is diminished by acting in a hostile, rejecting, or arrogant manner. Over time, actions speak louder than words, and a leader who tries to appear friendly but manipulates and exploits people will lose referent power (emphases mine).

Although each source of interpersonal power, used legally and ethically, is and should be part of the principal's interpersonal portfolio, clearly these five sources fall along a continuum of teacher resistance at one end to teacher commitment on the other. Hoy and Miskel (1996, p. 179) suggest that referent and expert power are most likely to foster teacher commitment while coercive power is most likely to foment teacher resistance. While legitimate and reward power are likely to gain teacher compliance, they are less likely to gain teacher commitment than expert or referent power.

What are the practical implications of these sources of interpersonal power? ***First,*** all are legitimate uses of interpersonal influence if done so legally, ethically, and in accordance with the mission of the school. In particular, contingency leadership theories (e.g., Fiedler's Contingency Theory, Hersey's and Blanchard's Situational Theory of Leadership) suggest there are situations in which principal behaviors emanating from legitimate, reward, and coercive power are necessary to gain staff compliance with facets of the school's mission. For example, a principal who comes in new to a building may be under pressure from the superintendent and the school board to "turn around" the school in a short time. Turning things around might entail raising poor standardized test scores, and the principal might have the blessing and the latitude of the superintendent and the board to issue directives to turn things around. Moreover, the principal might have the latitude to reward compliers and punish noncompliers. In addition, a new principal with this task probably does not have the time to immediately establish expert and referent power. ***Second,*** interpersonal power should not be seen as a method for constraining subordinates (Hoy & Miskel, 1996). For example, principals with specialized knowledge that teachers need would be foolish not to share this knowledge. Hoarding knowledge is clearly a means of control; even worse, hoarding knowledge cheats teachers of opportunities to exercise autonomy in their work, and in some cases is unethical, if not illegal. ***Third,*** over the long run, principals and other leaders who depend predominantly on power flowing from the organization will foster teacher resistance and alienation. Teachers are professionals and should be trusted and treated as such until the trust is breached. By application then, principals who rely on expert and referent power are more likely to gain teacher commitment. To be viewed as experts, principals must continually update their knowledge and skills and model these behaviors to teachers. To exercise referent influence, principals must possess characteristics like those mentioned by Yukl (1989) in the quoted passage on the previous page. An elaboration of many of these characteristics is provided in the next section.

PORTFOLIO OF PERSONAL TRAITS

Extensive reading (see, for example, Blase & Blase, 1994; Blase & Kirby, 1992; Brodinsky, 1983; Fox, 1986; Hoy & Miskel, 1996; Lortie, 1975; Rosenholtz, 1989; Yukl, 1989), some experience, and conversations with principals have led me to compile a portfolio of personal traits that are essential for principals to possess to enhance their ability to increase referent (true interpersonal) power. Two considerations are important: (1) No particular "personality" is necessary to possess these traits (a low key person can be just as likely to display these traits as a "rah-rah" person), and (2) this list is by no means exhaustive. For the sake of organization, I have taken the liberty to classify these traits into six general categories; however, the categories are not as important as the traits themselves. Here goes.

- **Integrity**. Defined as the "Rigid adherence to a code or standard of values" (*American Heritage Dictionary*, 1982), integrity is listed as the first category of personal traits for a reason. It connotes fidelity to a standard of values. This standard of values must be personal and organizational (fidelity to "what is good," the mission of the school, the betterment of kids, etc.). To me, integrity comprises fairness, honesty, and trustworthiness. Fairness mandates that we be equitable in our dealings with those with whom we come into contact. Honesty is just what is means, whether it is involved in recognizing effective performance, suggesting means for improvement, or reprimanding. Trustworthiness has three connotations. *First*, it connotes trust in one's own abilities. *Second*, it connotes the degree to which the teaching staff can trust the principal. *Third*, it connotes the ability of the principal to trust the staff. In my opinion, no one of these three can exist apart from the other two.

  Stephen Covey (1989) uses the metaphor "Emotional Bank Account" (p. 188) to describe the trust that you build with another person. In each interpersonal interaction, you make a deposit to or withdrawal from this account. With each deposit you make, the account reserve becomes greater and the level of trust in the other person places in you becomes higher. If you make a withdrawal, you decrease the account reserve and lower the level of trust another person has in you.

  To build this account and teachers' levels of trust , Covey (pp. 190-198) suggests that you strive to make the following six deposits:

  - **Understand the individual**
  - **Attend to the little things**
  - **Keep commitments**
  - **Clarify expectations**

- **Show personal integrity**
- **Apologize sincerely when you make a withdrawal.**

Finally, two quotations that sum up the meaning of integrity. The first comes from Dr. Gordon Anderson, Superintendent of Spring Independent School District, who once said at one a beginning-of-school meeting, "When you tell someone you're going to do something, do it." The second comes from former Texas Governor Richard Coke, who uttered over a century ago:

"Let your watchword be duty, and know no other talisman of success than labor. Let honor be your guiding star in your dealings with your superiors, your fellows, with all. Be as true to a trust reposed as the needle to the pole, stand by the right even to the sacrifice of life itself, and learn that death is preferable to dishonor."

Strong words, to be sure. But they capture the essence of integrity.

- **Confidence**. Confidence is another word that connotes many things. At a minimum, it connotes:
  - *Self-confidence.* True self-confidence should not be confused with arrogance. Self-confidence connotes confidence in one's knowledge, skills, and abilities. Self-confidence is not something that can be faked for long; without something to be confident in, the mask of self-confidence is quickly removed in the eyes of the teaching staff and becomes arrogance. In addition, self-confident principals are more likely to establish high goals, take on difficult tasks, be more persistent (Hoy & Miskel, 1996), and see the big picture. As we have alluded to earlier, a self-confident principal must continually update and refine knowledge, skills, and abilities. Finally, truly self-confident principals acknowledge when they have made mistakes (in other words, can say "I was wrong") and, as importantly, learn from mistakes.

- *Confidence in others.* Confidence in others is readily self-defining. A principal who displays confidence in teachers views teachers as professionals who have professional and personal needs for growth (see our discussion of Theory Y in Chapter 1). Principals who are able to display confidence in teachers: (1) Seek teachers who are eminently qualified, (2) set and communicate teacher expectations and goals, (3) grant teachers the autonomy necessary to attain expectations, (4) encourage teachers to be innovative, and (5) understand that teachers make mistakes. At the same, principals who display confidence in teachers are not threatened by teachers' knowledge, skills, and abilities. Principals who display this confidence constantly express this confidence to the teaching staff, students, and community.
- *Optimism.* I place optimism in this category, although it could go elsewhere. There is a lot of pessimism in schools today. Optimism is not positive thinking without justification, but rather "non-negative thinking" (Seligman, 1991, p. 222) with justification. While acknowledging the challenges incumbent in schooling, confident principals see the glass as "half full" rather than "half empty." Confident principals do not "blow sunshine," but believe that tasks are capable of being accomplished and provide the leadership and resources necessary to do so.
- *Enthusiasm.* As a corollary to optimism, confident principals are enthusiastic about their work. This enthusiasm does not have to be evidenced as "cheerleader" enthusiasm; indeed, low-key principals can also be enthusiastic. Principals manifest their enthusiasm through their own motivation and dedication and by treating and supporting teachers as colleagues (Blase & Blase, 1994). Enthusiastic principals, by words and actions, convey to teach-

ers the feeling that they can attain even the most challenging of goals.

- *Energy and initiative*. Initiative means the trait of being a self-starter and not having to be told what to do and how to do it. Energy suggests physical, intellectual, and emotional drive and stamina. Both are necessary to be confident as a principal
- *Common sense*. Again, this trait could be classified elsewhere. Common sense is the ability of the principal to exercise sound judgment (see the volume on "Judgment" in *The School Leadership Library*). Principals with common sense do not rush to make a decision when an immediate decision is not necessary, reflect on their actions and during their actions, understand legal and ethical parameters of decision-making, and do not promise more than they can deliver.

♦ **Approachability**. Teachers feel they can approach principals who are:

- *Friendly*. No one likes to approach a principal with a concern or a problem and get his or her head bitten off. Friendly, approachable principals put teachers at ease and foster in teachers the willingness to voice concerns, make suggestions, and experience ownership in the school's mission.
- *Accessible and visible*. Inaccessibility and low visibility are sure signs that the principal is unapproachable. While principals are required at times to retire to the office and close the door, there is a difference between this behavior and never coming out of the office. In addition to being traits of approachability, the principal's accessibility and visibility also tell teachers that the principal is concerned with what is going on in the building. Finally, accessibility and visibility provide teachers with a sense of security.
- *Able and willing to listen*. As the leader of the school, principals are expected to be there and listen to the

victories, successes, concerns, and complaints of teachers. Sometimes, teachers (as well as students and parents) just need someone on whom to unload. Principals who are willing and able to listen as well as able to offer consolation, advice, and encouragement will be far more approachable than those who are unwilling or unable. It goes with the territory!

- **Consideration**. In the language of leadership theory, consideration is described as principals' behavior that displays trust, friendship, interest, and respect toward teachers (Halpin, 1966). It is appropriately the affective side of leader behavior, as opposed to the task-oriented side of leader behavior. Consideration can be thought of to comprise the following the traits:
  - *Care and concern*. Considerate principals express interest and concern for the professional and personal problems of teachers, for the challenges teachers face in their work, for the well-being of students, and for the triumphs of teachers. Principals express this care and concern by modeling many of the behaviors noted under "Approachability." In addition, principals act on their care and concern to provide supportive resources and recognition, as appropriate to the situation.
  - *Supportiveness*. Principals consistently display their support for teachers' challenges, concerns, and victories. Whether providing a word of encouragement, a suggestion or directive for professional development, public recognition, or financial or material resources necessary for teachers to attain goals, supportive principals are in tune to the needs of teachers and are there to offer the support necessary for teachers to meet their challenges.
  - *Tactfulness*. Tactfulness is the "sensitivity to what is appropriate at any given time in. . . relationships, together with the ability to speak or act without offense" (*American Heritage Dictionary*, 1982, p. 1237). Even when faced with the unpleasant task of

reprimanding teachers, tactful principals do so by focusing on the undesirable behavior rather than on the personality, thereby enabling the teacher to retain his or her dignity. Tact is not, however, masking the truth.

- **Tolerance**. Principals who wish to referently influence teachers are tolerant. At a minimum, tolerance includes:
  - *Tolerance for ambiguity*. The ambiguity or uncertainty of a principal's job is manifest in many ways. For example, principals may plan out the activities for an entire day to make sure that what is important gets done. On walking into the office, they may be confronted by unexpected and certainly unplanned situations. Perhaps the parents of an elementary school student are upset because their son or daughter did not get to sing a solo in the spring concert. I can remember from personal experience planning to observe a teacher during first period and walking into my office to find two students who had just fought each other, parents who were upset that their son was excluded from a band concert because of his involvement with the baseball team, and a teacher with a concern that just could not wait. The "best-laid" plans often do not turn out the way you hoped. Of course, many individual tasks are also ambiguous by nature. Take, for instance, trying to resolve a child custody case involving an elementary school student, investigating peer sexual harassment claims of secondary school students, or developing a professional growth plan with a teacher. By their very nature, these activities are not accompanied by a "cookbook" solution that works the same every time. Simply put, a person with little tolerance for ambiguity is not well suited for the principalship.
  - *Tolerance for stress*. A corollary to tolerance for ambiguity is the tolerance for stress. You know as well as I that the stress associated with being a principal or assistant principal is at times overwhelming. The

hours and pace of work are at times exhausting. At certain times of the year, the stress is particularly acute (the beginning and end of school, for example). Principals who exhibit a high tolerance for stress are better decision makers, provide better direction to the staff, and provide the expectation that stress is something with which to be dealt. In fact, principals are obligated to "check their stress at the door" and, at the same time, are obligated to address the obvious stresses that teachers face.

- *Patience.* Tolerant principals are patient as they address the myriad of issues that surface daily. They have ice water in their veins outwardly, even if they are boiling inwardly. Although patience is tested daily, tolerant principals rarely, if ever, become impatient in their interpersonal dealings.
- *Emotional maturity.* Tolerant principals are emotionally mature and are not given to emotional peaks and valleys. Principals are expected to be the "rocks" of the school, there every day, ready to go, enthusiastic, visible, approachable, and confident. At the same time, principals are expected to be the rocks on which teachers lean, particularly in times of crisis. In addition, emotionally mature principals are improvement oriented and are objective about their strengths and weaknesses (Hoy & Miskel, 1996).
- *Sense of humor.* Although I saved this trait for last, it might be one of the top two or three personal traits necessary to flourish in the principalship. Principals with a sense of humor see the "light" side of challenges and issues that they face. More importantly, they are able to laugh at themselves and not take themselves too seriously. A sense of humor suggests to others a certain level of vulnerability and fallibility (which is present in all of us, whether we admit it to ourselves or not) and is often the only way to cope with the challenges that principals face. To wit, "Laff every time you pheel tick-

led, and laff once in awhile anyhow" (Josh Billings, in Prochnow & Prochnow, 1964, p. 398). Finally:

> If we consider the frequent reliefs we receive from laughter, and how often it breaks the gloom which is apt to depress the mind, one would take care not to grow too wise for so great a pleasure of life. (Addison, in Prochnow & Prochnow, 1964, p. 398)

TWENTY QUESTIONS

Well, there it is. Superwoman or Superman disguised as a principal? No, not at all. Only a caring educator who believes in what is good and decent and models these beliefs in his or her interpersonal words and actions.

How well do you measure up? We all have played the game twenty questions. As often as not, the game is played to elicit the truth (from time to time I played the game with high school students to determine their innocence or guilt when they had been accused of misbehavior!) from the person subjected to the questions. I have chosen to end this volume with twenty questions for you to pose to yourself regarding the collection of materials in your "Portfolio of One." Many of these questions are based on the work of Evelyn Horn (1991); others I have written to get at other facets of the portfolio. Remember, when we examine ourselves, we have all the facts. Without further comment, here goes.

- Do I structure teaching assignments and activities to give teachers a greater sense of challenge and responsibility?
- Am I confident enough in myself and my teaching staff to encourage them to experiment and try new teaching methods, even if they fail at first?
- Am I enthusiastic about being leader of this building? If not, how can I become enthusiastic?
- Do I subscribe to educational journals and read widely enough to keep current in the field?
- Am I willing to make it possible for all teachers in my building to succeed and to give them recognition on a regular basis? Am I honest and tactful enough to give

constructive criticism after laying a foundation of trust between myself and the teachers?

- Am I willing to ask for help from teachers and fellow principals who seem to be more successful than I am? Do I actually observe them first hand?
- Do I foster teacher autonomy wherever possible so that teachers feel they are responsible for the outcomes of their work?
- When things are going well and students and teachers are in a flow, do I leave it alone?
- Am I perceived by my staff as having integrity and displaying trust in my staff? Do I have these qualities?
- Am I perceived by my staff as fair and equitable in my dealings with teachers? Am I?
- If a teacher performs poorly, do I consider my role and responsibility instead of immediately blaming the teacher? At the same time, do I possess the knowledge, skills, and trust to assist teachers who are not meeting expectations and, if necessary, the courage to remove the teacher for the sake of students?
- Do I show genuine consideration for teachers, particularly those who seem to have little outside support?
- Am I perceived by my staff as knowledgeable about the teaching and learning process? Am I?
- Am I perceived by my staff as approachable and helpful? Am I?
- Am I perceived by my staff as accessible and visible? Am I?
- Am I perceived by my staff as a good listener? Am I?
- Am I perceived by my teachers as tolerant of ambiguity, stress, and the concerns that they bring to me on a daily basis?
- Does my teaching staff view me as encouraging and supportive? Do I take advantage of every opportunity to publicly and individually express my confidence in my staff and the important jobs they are doing?
- Does my staff view me as optimistic? Do my actions speak for themselves?
- Do I display a sense of humor? Am I able to laugh at myself?

References

American heritage dictionary (2nd College Edition) (1982). Boston, MA: Houghton Mifflin.

Ashford, S.J. (1986). Feedback-seeking in individual adaptation: A resource perspective. *Academy of Management Journal, 29,* 465–487.

Barnard, C.I. (1938). *Functions of an executive.* Cambridge, MA: Harvard University Press.

Bartell, C.A. (1987). *Incentives that enhance the teaching profession: Background paper.* Elmhurst, IL: North Central Regional Educational Laboratory. (ERIC Document Reproduction Service No. ED 326 994)

Blase, J., & Blase, J.R. (1994). *Empowering teachers: What successful principals do.* Newbury Park, CA: Corwin Press.

Blase, J., & Kirby, P.C. (1992). *Bringing out the best in teachers: What effective principals do.* Newbury Park, CA: Corwin Press.

Borg, W.R., Gall, J.P., & Gall, M.D. (1993). *Applying educational research: A practical guide* (3rd ed.). New York: Longman.

Brandt, R. (1995). Punished by rewards?: A conversation with Alfie Kohn. *Educational Leadership, 53,* 13–16.

Bridges, E.M. (1967). A model for shared decision-making in the school principalship. *Educational Administration Quarterly, 3,* 49–61.

Brodinsky, B. (1983). *Building morale...motivating staff: Problems and solutions.* Arlington, VA: American Association of School Administrators.

Brewer, E.W., Achilles, C.M., & Fuhriman, J.R. (1995). *Finding funding: Grantwriting and project management from start to finish* (2nd ed.). Thousand Oaks, CA: Corwin Press.

Covey, S.R. (1989). *The 7 habits of highly effective people.* New York: Simon & Schuster.

Cresap, McCormick, & Paget, Inc. (1984). *Teacher incentives: A tool for effective management.* (A joint publication of the American Association of School Administrators, the National Association of Elementary School Principals, and the National Association of Secondary School Principals). Reston, VA: National Association of Secondary School Principals. (ERIC Document Reproduction Service No. ED 244 388)

Csikszentmihalyi, M. (1990). *Flow: The psychology of optimal experience*. New York: Harper & Row.

Daft, R.L. (1988). *Management*. New York: The Dryden Press.

Deci, E.L., & Ryan, R.M. (1985). *Intrinsic motivation and self-determination in human behavior*. New York: Plenum.

Fox, W.M. (1986, November). *Teacher motivation*. Paper presented at the Annual Conference of the National Council of States on Inservice Education, Nashville, LA. (ERIC Document Reproduction Service No. ED 275 677)

Frase, L.E. (1992). *Maximizing people power in schools: Motivating and managing teachers and staff*. Newbury Park, CA: Corwin Press.

French, J.R.P., & Raven, B.H. (1968). Bases of social power. In D. Cartwright and A. Zander (Eds.), *Group Dynamics: Research and Theory* (pp. 259–270). New York: Harper & Row.

Geen, R.G. (1995). *Human motivation: A social psychological approach*. Belmont, CA: Brooks/Cole Publishing Company.

Hackman, J.R., & Oldham, G.R. (1976). Motivation through the design of work: A test of a theory. *Organizational Behavior and Human Performance, 16*, 250–279.

Halpin, A.W. (1966). *Theory and research in administration*. New York: Macmillan.

Hersey, P., & Blanchard, K.H. (1977). *Management of organizational behavior: Utilizing human resources* (3rd ed.). Englewood Cliffs, NJ: Prentice-Hall.

Herzberg, F., Mausner, B., & Snyderman, B. (1959). *The motivation to work*. New York: John Wiley.

Horn, E.D. (1991). *An argument for using intrinsic rather than extrinsic motivation, with specific suggestions for teachers*. (ERIC Document Reproduction Service No. ED 355 036)

Howard, E.R., & Keefe, J.W. (1991). *The CASE-IMS school improvement process*. Reston, VA: National Association of Secondary School Principals.

Hoy, W.K., & Miskel, C.G. (1991). *Educational administration: Theory, research, practice* (4th ed.). New York: McGraw-Hill.

Hoy, W.K., & Miskel, C.G. (1996). *Educational administration: Theory, research, practice* (5th ed.). New York: McGraw-Hill.

Kaiser, J.S. (1982). Teacher longevity: Motivation and burnout. *Clearing House, 15* (1), 17–19.

Lieberman, A., & Miller, L. (1984). *Teachers, their world, and their work.* Alexandria, VA: Association for Supervision and Curriculum Development.

Locke, E.A., & Latham, G.P. (1990). *A theory of goal setting and task performance.* Englewood Cliffs, NJ: Prentice-Hall.

Lortie, D.C. (1975). *Schoolteacher: A sociological study.* Chicago: University of Chicago Press.

Maslow, A.H. (1954). *Motivation and personality.* New York: Harper & Row.

McGregor, D. (1960). *The human side of enterprise.* New York: McGraw-Hill.

Miskel, C., & Ogawa, R. (1988). Work motivation, job satisfaction, and climate. In N.J. Boyan (Ed.), *Handbook of Research in Educational Administration* (pp. 279-304). New York: Longman.

Owens, R.G. (1991). *Organizational behavior in education* (4th ed.). Boston, MA: Allyn & Bacon.

Owens, R.G. (1995). *Organizational behavior in education* (5th ed.). Boston, MA: Allyn & Bacon.

Peters, T. (1988). *Thriving on chaos: Handbook for a management revolution.* New York: Knopf.

Porter, L.W. (1961). A study of perceived need satisfactions in bottom and middle management jobs. *Journal of Applied Psychology, 45,* 1–10.

Prochnow, H.V., & Prochnow, H.V. (1964). *The public speaker's treasure chest* (2nd ed.). New York: Harper & Row.

Rodale, J.I. (1978). *The synonym finder.* Emmaus, PA: Rodale Press.

Rosenholtz, S.J. (1989). *Teachers' workplace: The social organization of schools.* New York: Longman.

Seligman, M.E. (1991). *Learned optimism.* New York: Knopf.

Sergiovanni, T.J. (1991). *The principalship: A reflective practice perspective* (2nd ed.). Boston: Allyn & Bacon.

Sergiovanni, T.J. (1995). *The principalship: A reflective practice perspective* (3rd ed.). Boston: Allyn & Bacon.

Sergiovanni, T.J. (1992). *Moral leadership: Getting to the hear of school improvement*. San Francisco, CA: Jossey-Bass Publishers.

Schmuck, R.A., & Runkel, P.J. (1994). *The handbook of organizational development in schools and colleges*. Prospect Heights, IL: Waveland Press.

Thompson, D.P. (1994, April). *Job satisfaction: A synthesis of research in the Educational Administration Quarterly*. Paper presented at the annual meeting of the American Educational Research Association, New Orleans, LA. (ERIC Document Reproduction Service No. ED 371 024)

Thomson, S.D. (Ed.). (1993). *Principals for our changing schools*. Fairfax, VA: National Policy Board for Educational Administration.

Vroom, V.H. (1964). *Work and motivation*. New York: John Wiley & Sons.

Yukl, G.A. (1989). *Leadership in organizations* (2nd ed.). Englewood Cliffs, NJ: Prentice-Hall.